How to Cheat
at
French Verbs

REMY OH

Other Books by this Author:

Orphans of Katrina: Inside the World's Biggest Animal Rescue. (Non-fiction)

The Really Red Rabbit. (A children's picture book)

The Writer and the Quail. (A comedy novella)

Rio's Favelas: An Insider Uncovers the Myths, the Music, the Murders. (Non-fiction)

THIRD EDITION
E-book and paperback
August 8th 2022
Second edition
June 9th 2020
Original edition
September 18^{th,} 2019

Give a Dog a Bone Press

Publisher:
Give a Dog a Bone Press
Playa del Rey, CA 90293

**Whether you think you can,
or think you can't –
you're right.**
Henry Ford

CONTENTS

INTRODUCTION

Introduction

If you love to rebel, hate memorizing verbs, and want to see the friendly side of French -- *bienvenue*. My goal is to get you up and running in *spoken* French so you can speak and understand the language as quickly as possible. And yes, that means cheating, using every tip, trick, secret and hack known to man -- and then mine.

Face it, foreign languages aren't friendly. They aren't. They can be real snobs, insisting that you learn their way of doing *everything*. They'll expect you to deal with their complex rules, endless vocabulary, and difficult pro-nunciation. You've got to absorb a whole new way of thinking just to say a simple sentence. They're *foreign* to *everything* you've already learned in a lifetime of speaking your own native language. (Foreign, from the Latin word *foris,* meaning *outside*.)

You'd think that French would be the height of language snobbery: a hoity-toity, wine sniffing, holier-than-thou form of expression. But its cold, harsh *façade* is all an act. *Français* is a warm, fun, *easy* language to learn. Yes, *easy*. It's a playful language full of quiet wallflowers looking for a dance partner, ultra-rebellious bad boys with superhero talents, a double agent, and of course, that crazy family of seven -- the tight-knit Kumbaya clan.

But first, grab your camouflage gear and slip on those Doc Martin boots -- we're going to war against French as it's taught today. We'll take a sledge-hammer to the status *boring* quo. Order a drone strike on every book of 501 verbs – *in any language*. And toss a live grenade at any past tense verb that even *hints* at being annoying – which would be all of them. We're talking major rule breaking here.

Together we'll rise up against the classic French verb charts that have been in effect since the 17th century. *Mon Dieu!*

Here we'll prove to any condescending grammar nerd that you don't have to know the difference between the plus perfect indicative, second person plu-ral, in the affirmative, and the past participle agreement, first person singular, in the negative, to order a *vin rouge* in a Paris café. (We spoke our native languages fluently, perfectly, effortlessly, before we even knew what a verb did.)

And together, here, we'll turn the French verb tables upside down (Literally.)

On your mark, get set – *cheat!*

But hold on. You might be thinking -- why should we change the status *bor-ing* quo? It's worked for millions of French learners for decades. Heck, cen-turies even.

Mais oui. Exactly. After centuries, anything could use a tweak. Especially *français.* Unlike other romance languages, French can be a lot more… friendly. It's got lots of tricks and secrets to help you beat the system. Trust me, I know them all. I invented most of them. (I'm a world-class conjugater hater.)

My full-scale grammar rebellion started innocently. I was at a Scottsdale, Arizona library book sale when I picked up a brand new, unopened French verb book on sale for two bucks. (Of course it was unopened. Who wants to study conjugation?)

My mind glazed over as I eyed the haughty verb charts. Oh, yes, the famous charts. Yawn. What a bore. Get a life verb charts.

So there I was, gazing at that familiar fog of repetitive words. *Je suis, tu es, il, elle, on est, nous sommes*… blah, blah, blah, when the same thought came to me that *always* came to me: hadn't anyone figured out that these charts were *wrong?* Was I the only one who realized that they made learning French *more* difficult? Surely *everyone* had noticed this by now. Hadn't they? I tossed the book back in the bin.

Sauntering off, I observed more library carts piled high with lonely, rejected books, each hoping to find a home. But my mind was focused on one thing: those snobby, complicated French verb charts.

They *couldn't* be wrong, could they? No. They'd been around forever. People dedicated years of their lives to memorizing them: smart people, Harvard professor types. Multi-lingual conjugation bloggers. Students with thick, black glasses who could spew out every tense in rocket speed French, backwards and forwards. Who was I to think these charts were nothing more than an ill planned, sketchy attempt to pass off difficult French verbs to a misguided public? Nah. The charts couldn't be wrong.

I went back to the sale bin and plucked out that same smug verb book. I rifled through the pages feeling pity for the centuries of people who had suffered, lost in these lists. But wait -- what if the charts *were* wrong? The fact that they had been around forever… well, maybe people took them for granted. Maybe *everyone* assumed that *someone else* had verified them, like all those smart people, the Harvard professor types. The multi-lingual conjugation bloggers. Or those students, with the thick, black glasses who…. well, you get the picture.

I peeled open the book to a painful chart, a complicated verb that I hated at first sight. Were the charts right or wrong? Was there a better way to arrange them? Could a *little* tweak fix enough of the verb conjugations to make a *big* difference? Yes, it could! Just a nip here and there and it would revolutionize French language learning. WOW! I was either a complete genius (like my mother always said,) or just plain nuts (like my father always said.)

I had to know. I called up a friend, a Parisian *belle*, a long time French teacher. "Hi Coco, can you do me a favor? Can you put some thought into the layout of those very unfriendly French conjugation charts?"

"*Comment?*" she said. I bet her head spun around like she was cast in *The Exorcist.*

"The verb charts," I said. "You know, like in those books, *501 French Verbs.* Can you look at the order? The crazy way they arranged the charts. I'm sure they can be improved. It would be much easier to learn French if those silly charts were fixed."

Coco didn't answer. There was an extended silence. She was either thoughtfully analyzing the charts in her mind– or she was Googling the local psych ward.

"Those *silly* charts were approved by the French Academy," she snapped. "They are the perfect, appropriate, time-honored, valuable means to convey the true conjugation of French verbs in all tenses, at all times. (Never challenge a Parisian about French, or about Camembert cheese, for that matter).

Hmm, what if Coco was drinking the Kool Aid, too. She had taught these charts for decades. Like everyone else, maybe she'd taken them for granted. After all – they were backed by the "French Academy," whatever that was. Could everyone be so programmed by memorizing these same, annoying charts -- that no one questioned them? These boring charts were apparently locked in stone; the holy grail of things I wanted to eviscerate.

"So, this French Academy?" I said.

Another long pause from Coco's end. Uh-oh. Would the grammar police be scurrying to my front door wearing crisp white uniforms, yelling into a bullhorn: "Surrender on behalf of French speakers everywhere." You must learn *le bon usage.* You will not destroy our language. Oh and, you really should mow your lawn."

Coco finally responded in her weathered accent; she musta been reading from Wikipedia...

"The French Academy was founded in 1635. The main task has always been to work with as much care and diligence as possible to give fixed rules to our beautiful language and to make sure it remains pure, eloquent, and capable of treating this fabled language of our world, the language of the arts and the sciences, with dignity. Any change to the *subtilties* of French grammar is a destruction of our very existence, the demise of our core! As Albert Camus once said 'The French language is my homeland.'"

"So—you're not a fan of changing the verb charts?"

Silence. I imagined three elegant men back in the year 1635. They were sipping café from translucent, bone china cups, their pinkies extended. Theylooked ridiculous in their long grey wigs and silk culottes as they discussed *les bons mots*, within the gloomy Academy.

"Coco, what if I changed very little? We're talking hiccup size, a snip here -, there. Minor. Coco? Hello. You there? Hello, hello…"

Coco was gone.

Okay, I got it. If I dared venture into this French Neverland by performing a hem job on the charts, the Academy would be chasing me down the Champs-Élysées with bayonets and verb-filled parchment manuscripts shouting: "*Arrêtez, arrêtez*! Traitor! *Traitresse*! How dare you -- *you're not even French*!" Coco would be at the head of the pack, leading them through the gathering crowds. *Mon Dieu*! Would a guillotine be next?

Damn. Would *anyone* be on my side about this? I figured, even if others, somewhere, realized that these charts could be improved – who would bother to fix them? Would anyone dare picket outside of the French Academy? Was anyone insane enough to rewrite 384 years of confusing verb history? Who would be so crazy, so outlandish, so arrogant, so incensed, so off-their-rocker, that they'd go after the entire French speaking world? Was *anyone* that nuts?

Wait -- I was! And heck, while I was stirring up verbs, I figured I might as well challenge *everything* about learning French! (Why must I go *all in* about every issue? Maybe my father was right.) French should be a fast, fun, easy language to learn. Friendly. Approachable. And it can be.

You still with me? Here we are, a *troupe* of grammar haters, rebelling against the entire verb infused establishment. We're all on that fabulous 'rule breaking, picketing, fists-in-the-air, Che Guevara T-shirt wearing, rebel team.' Hip-hip-hooray for us.

PART ONE

Welcome to Frenchville:
the Land of Superheroes,
Wallflowers, Missing Links,
and
Other Tall Tales.

One

So who's this book for, anyway?

This book is directed at beginning French students. Or an intermediate who wants a refresher, or like us, who prefers to cheat rather than memorize complex verb charts. Or for travelers who want to get the most out of their trip.

If you're at the stage where you've looked into a bit of vocabulary... and you know who these people are: *je, tu, il, elle, on, nous, vous, ils, elles*... and you're dabbling in the world of verbs, this little guide will get you up and running quickly. If you're past that stage, and you know tons of verbs already, stick with us, there are lots more than just verbs in this book.

In about a month of leisurely thinking, using your imagination, and being a tad creative -- you'll be speaking friendly French faster than earthly possible. Keep picking up vocabulary and expressions as we go, and I'll help you with that – and your verb conjugation – my style of conjugation.

I've chosen 50 of the most useful French verbs and the short cut to learning them. You will *never* find yourself staring at that infamous French Academy charts, or memorizing 501 verbs *ad nauseum*. Instead, you can be out buying avocados, returning a T-shirt to Macys, or driving your *petit chien* to the doggie park – and you'll be studying French the whole time. Whatever you do, wherever you are, you can easily advance, even with no books or CD's within in reach. (Dang, I'm setting a pretty high bar for myself.) With these

50 most used verbs, in 4.5 tenses, you'll be conversing in smart French everywhere.

And keep in mind, I'm gonna drum-up every trick I know. Tons of new info will be jetting in. But don't get worried. Grab the parts you want to learn right now. Don't overwhelm yourself thinking there's soooo much to remember. You're fine. We all learn piece-by-piece. The details are here so you always have them to refer to. Learning languages is a *process*. That is, a *series* of actions and steps taken to achieve an end.

Relax. French is easy to learn.

Really. It's easy to learn.

For many people studying languages can be stressful. From where you stand at the beginning, there is a vast, rocky, unknown territory stretched out before you. You're on foot, alone, limping along, might have a pebble stuck in your shoe, and maybe you're lugging a heavy backpack weighed down with a lifetime of doubt. Can you even learn a language? Will you give up half way? Will you convince yourself that you're not smart enough? Are you too old? Too young? Will you become so overwhelmed that you never want to hear the word *baguette* again?

The great thing about learning languages is you cannot go backwards. Every time you learn even one word, you've moved forward. ONE WORD puts you ahead. Word by word, with every little phrase, every word set, you're better off than you were just one word before. We're talking *a word* here. A bunch of little letters glued together. Sounds. Just one little word, and the magical land of language is opening up to you. Runners may have to sweat over *miles* to officially get somewhere. Accountants may have *piles* of taxes to weed through to get ahead. A proctologist may have to, well, never mind.

We're talking words here. Combinations of letters. Sounds.

By the time you were five years old you were practically *fluent* in your native language. You were five years old. FIVE. You'd never even heard of a prepositional phrase yet there you were spewing out perfect English, or German, or Chinese. Just five and you aced it. Why was it so easy? It was easy because a child is focused. They will learn exactly what THEYneed to know as THEY need it. They will not start out learning about verb conjugations, accent marks, and adjectives. They learn just what they need, as they need it. Their first words are mommy, daddy, juice, go, no, yes, bye, hi. These are the important in their world.

Learning languages summed up in one word: YOU

Surprise, when learning a language, the focus isn't on the language at all – the focus is on YOU! Language is all about YOU. Your travels. Your personality. Your needs. Your world. French is here for you -- to focus on what YOU need.

Languages were developed to serve the user. Always remember that. They were developed over centuries to allow people to communicate. You don't need to know all the words and all the conjugations. You only need to know what YOU need to know for your life, your needs. How can language serve you?

It's easy to see a new language like you're entering a dark forest, where you'll easily get lost, and you'll find giant, growling bears hiding around every pine, ready to chase you off. But no.

You don't have to roll-up your sleeves and enter what seems to be endless black woods. Just the opposite. Languages have to roll-up *their* sleeves and go to work FOR YOU. They are here to serve YOU. It's not a forest -- it's an open field. YOUR field, tailored for you, at your speed, for your needs. YOU ARE THE BOSS. You choose what you want and need to learn. Don't stress. Chop down all the unnecessary trees. Learn the basics. The top used verbs. The most valuable basic words. (Google the 100, 250 and even 500 top frequency words.) You're not at the mercy of a new language. A language doesn't even exist without the all important - YOU.

Here are two questions:

Why do you want to learn French?

Where are you going with your new language skills?

Why are you learning French? Are you just curious? A high school promise to yourself? An upcoming trip to Europe?

Where are you taking your new language? To French class? On a cruise? To help you speak with your French *amour*?

You're in charge here. What words do YOU need the most to communicate right away? Will you start out in the countryside? You might learn cows, horses, farm, sunflowers, tractor, irrigation, poppies, corn, insects, etc. Will you be on a coast? Focus on sailboat, current, shore, seashells, dock, horizon, waves, sunburn, etc. Are you staying home, studying French? Learn words about schools, family, pets, neighborhoods, books, etc.

FOCUS on YOU. What are your needs?

Simply put – never let a language scare you. It has no power over you. It's just here to help you. 100% here to help YOU. So don't be afraid.

And that 5-year old... where is that little kid who had no fear? Where is that little guy who shrugged when he messed up? That budding linguist hasn't gone anywhere.

Recently I met a 37-year old Mexican landscaper, Javier. He had no education, left school in Oaxaca in the 4th grade to stay home with his ailing mother. Moving to the US, he worked in the watermelon fields for 9 years, surrounded only by Spanish speakers. He spent another three years laboring in an apple orchard, again, surrounded by Spanish speakers.

He spoke perfect English. *Perfect English.* He never had videos to watch; no CD's to play; he didn't learn in a classroom full of students planning their next trip abroad. He had a ripped, pocket sized English/Spanish dictionary and a bag full of outdated Reader's Digests. He would study the articles over and over, looking up everything until he understood the word, the sentence, the paragraph, the page. WORD. SENTENCE. PARAGRAPH. PAGE.

For whatever reasons, for his own reasons, Javier was motivated to learn. And I believe that, and only that, *motivation*, will decide how far you go with a language. So there is no such thing as failing at learning a language. You're not a failure. It's not your age, your IQ, your ability to catch flying verbs at the speed of light. Not learning a language is never a personal failure in anyway. You just weren't motivated enough anymore. No self-flagellation involved in language learning. Don't stress. This is gonna be easy. Promise!

WORD. SENTENCE. PARAGRAPH. PAGE.

Learning to speak is the most important use of a new language, but reading is a great way to help you get there, even starting with children's books or later, teen books. Here are tricks to getting the most out of it.

Be selective in what you read. Take the time to find topics that you're obsessed with understanding. Read about subjects you're passionate about. I've picked up a hundred French articles and books that I've never finished. I didn't look up *one* word. I didn't learn *one* thing.

If I'm reading something that I can't put down -- a topic that I am *desperate* to learn about (diamond heists) then no amount of translation or dictionary usage will annoy me. I'll look up everything. I *must* understand what it says. I'll learn every new word. Every new phrase. (Did you know that all diamonds are from 1 billion to 3.5 billion years old, and were formed over 100 miles down in earth's mantle?)

Besides reading about your favorite subjects in French, collect all the French writings you can. You'll need them for a fun game we'll check out later, WORD SAFARI, which I invented for us.

Read out loud whenever possible. Reading is a passive activity, but reading out loud engages you, makes it active. It will help your mouth form the words, you can hear your accent, work on it, and it'll train your brain to communicate in new terms. Google translate has pretty good pronunciation, plug in some sentences and listen. (BTW: 80% of all diamonds are sold in NYC. I don't wear them, I just like their heist stories.)

You're not learning English made for French people.

It's easy to get frustrated learning another language. In romance languages things can seem backwards, inside out, upside down. Words, phrases… the entire language might seem off kilter from your norm. It's *so* reasonable for us to say *white house,* but come on… house white? *Maison blanche*? Why? But they're not speaking English, in a French way. They are speaking French, in a French way. And it was created with zero regard for how English would be formed. Repeat: zero regard. (We'll get back to the *maison blanche* in a second.)

It's common for language learners to rely on their native language to speak another. "I say this in English, so this must be correct in French." It's not! First thing you must do is forget your English, Russian, or Chinese. *You're not speaking your language using French words.* You're entering a new world, a new culture, a new way of thinking... and it comes with its very own form of expression. Allow French to be itself. *C'est génial!*

But here's the trap when studying languages -- it's easy to hold yourself back, feeling awkward when repeating the bizarre new words and expressions you're learning. And these quirky expressions, in all languages *are everywhere.* Your own language seemed so much smarter, simpler, and more functional. Your own language is just so *normal* and comfortable compared to their crazy way of communicating.

Let's look at crazy *français.* To convey excitement, the French often say, "*Ah, la vache!*" (Oh, my cow!) Crazy expression, no? But you might have heard, or said, "Holy cow!" and never thought it was odd.

"*Je deviens chèvre!*" (I'm becoming a goat!) That means I'm going nuts. Becoming a goat? How odd. But wait, we're going *nuts*? Will we become cashews or pecans? We can also be *driven crazy.* Do we drive ourselves or call an Uber?

Then there's "*Chercher la petite bête.*" (Looking for the little beast.) That's someone looking for the petty difference in things. But while they're looking for the little beast – we're *splitting hairs.*

Point is, never censor a new language or yourself when speaking it. Go with the flow. Don't avoid their common expressions because you think you'll sound foolish. You won't. And there's a reason I'm focusing on the importance of French sayings – they're used constantly. As in all languages, as in your own, you'd be shocked if you realized how often you throw in idiomatic expressions.

Let's look at English *as a native French speaker.* English can be super *bizarre.* The basic words we use daily, the norm for us, our typical phrases -- stop foreigners *dead in their tracks.* (*Dead in their tracks?*)

Take our word *pretty.* A simple word. Seems innocent enough. *Pretty.* But look at how it's used everywhere.

"He's a pretty bad driver." "She's pretty sick." "That squirrel in the road is pretty dead." A French person learning English might say, "*Mais non! Impossible!* Pretty means *belle, beau,* lovely, attractive. Why shove the word *pretty* in the middle of a sentence describing a bad driver, a sick girl, a dead squirrel? Why would they throw it randomly in the middle of *any* sentence? *Mon Dieu! C'est fou!*"

I'm *pretty sure,* that any *pretty good* English speaker, finds it *pretty* normal to sprinkle the word *pretty* into *pretty* much every conversation – *pretty* much all the time. It's one of the great things about learning languages, you'll realize so much about your own language. You'll notice the creative words and expressions that you've taken for granted for years.

English is a maze of colorful, descriptive phrases. Of course *rubbernecking* simply means to slow down to observe an accident. Simple. But to an English learner, they'll see the word for what it really is: rubbernecking, our necks stretch way out, like made of rubber, to get a closer look. *Skyscraper,* it just means tall building. But stand at the base of any towering building looking straight up and it'll appear to scrape the clouds as they roll past. How about, "I can't get a word in edgewise?" Even if I grabbed a word, and turned it *edgewise* and tried to slip it in that way – I *still* couldn't fit it into conversation.

We *kick the bucket, break a leg, knock on wood, spill the beans, blow off steam* and take *cat naps.* We have *green thumbs,* get *under the weather,* and *jump in the shower.* (Have you ever *jumped* in?) We get *head over heels, ruffle feathers, let the cat out of the bag,* and like to *stay in the loop.* We even drive on parkways, and park in driveways.

You can see why foreigners can get dumbfounded by English. It's rife with pronunciation pitfalls, and spellings that are real head scratchers: (Dumbfounded? Pitfalls? Head scratchers?) Here are some English language stunners:

That *bear* is losing fur. I can't *bear* to see a *bare bear.*

I need to *read* what I already *read* in that *red* book.

Excuse me, but there's no *excuse* for that.

They're over *there* with *their* friends.

I'm not *content* with this *content*.

The *lead* ingredient is *lead*, or that's what I've been *led* to believe.

I'll never walk down the *aisle* on the *isle* of Hawaii.

And look at *phony bologna* to see a pronunciation and spelling headache.

Now back to the *maison blanche*. When I was learning my first romance language (Spanish) it seemed odd, out of place, to switch the description of an object, the adjective, to the end of the word set. Why? *White house* seems so much smarter than *maison blanche*. But one day I had a revelation -- if I were in the ocean, and there was a shark coming at me – it would be *way better* for someone to yell "*SHARK!*" than to yell "GRAY!" Maybe they were right putting the big ticket item first and *then* giving the details. *House white* suddenly made more sense than *white house*.

Introducing the bad boys.

Here are two very important points that you must grasp before we move on. Just two simple things. This first one you might already know, but bear with me, I'm going somewhere with this…

You've probably learned that there are three major verb endings in French: ER, IR, and RE. Well, not here.

Here we have 4 endings: ER, IR, RE, and the rest -- I call them the bad boys. These stubborn, mischievous, up-all-night, irregular guys throw all the rules out of the *fenêtre*. Everybody hates these dudes because they follow a different pattern than the rest of the verbs. They beat to their own *tambours*. We're talking rebels. Okay, so ER, IR, RE, and the bad boys. (Bad boys are my favs, and they'll even turn into superheroes at times.)

But hold on a sec. Why pull them out? Why not leave them in the group with all the rest of their verbs and just learn them? Well, because -- they're not like all the rest. They make the entire group look difficult to approach and unruly. A verb group is a like band of wild horses. All unique individuals within, yet they live together peacefully. But in their midst a juvenile male grows up and becomes rowdy, obstinate, begins to sow his wild oats, literally. The band will toss him out, turn their backs on him. And once again they'll live peacefully.

Looking at the group of ERs, IRs, REs, with their hundreds of words, and all their exceptions, it's easy to see them as a maze of booby trapped, complex verb categories, full of stallions kicking up their heels. Pull out these few exceptions, and you've got three very chill, manageable, friendly verb groups without a landmine in sight. Nothing to worry about. (Wait till you meet *ALLER* who was thrown out of the ER group -- he will love being compared to a wild stallion.) We're gonna chill out these verb groups so we can stop thinking of them as an unruly 'band on the run.' (Can you hear that Paul McCartney song?)

Don't tell me. Let me guess.

Here's a quiz: Please read the following charts. What's so special about these lists? (Don't worry about memorizing anything, not important now. If you already know them, great.)

PARLER (To speak/to talk)
Je parle
Tu parles
Il parle
Elle parle
On parle
Ils parlent
Elles parlent

Besides the fact that the *NOUS* and *VOUS* are missing from above, what's so interesting about this list? Many of you probably know – but the answer is one of the most important tricks to learning French.
How about this next list? What's so special about these 7 items?

15

MANGER (To eat)
Je mange
Tu manges
Il mange
Elle mange
On mange
Ils mangent
Elles mangent

Do you know what I'm looking for? Have you figured out the answer?
One more chance. How about *this* list:

AIMER (To love/to like)
J'aime
Tu aimes
Il aime
Elle aime
On aime
Ils aiment
Elles aiment

What is it about these three lists that make them so important for learning French quickly?

Yes, they're all ER regular verb endings.

Yes, they're all in the present tense. (Tense just means "time.")

Yes, the *nous* and *vous* have vanished. Yes, you may have noticed that *je aime* became *j'aime*. (This liaison makes it sounds smoother.)

But…. drum roll… what makes them super special is that ALL of these ER present tense verbs, associated with ALL of these personal pronouns, for ALL of these different people, or groups -- *are ALL pronounced exactly the same way*. MIND BLOWN. From the simple E ending, to the ES, to the whole ENT enchilada. They've all been through the famous French "letter dump" so they're all pronounced the same. WHAT?

All those words, in all those charts above, make only three sounds:

PARL... MANG... AIM...

1. **PARLER**: *Je **parle**, Tu **parles**, Il, Elle, On **parle**, Ils, Elles **parlent**.*

    ALL PRONOUNCED **PARL**

2. **MANGER**: *Je **mange**, Tu **manges**, Il, Elle, On **mange**, Ils, Elles **mangent**.*

    ALL PRONOUNCED **MANG.**

3. **AIMER**: *J'**aime**, Tu **aimes**, Il, Elle, On **aime**, Ils, Elles **aiment**.*

    ALL PRONOUNCED **AIM.**

Letter dump here we come! Now we can learn tons of ER verbs easily. Tons! Over 1000 ER verbs – conquered easily. Boom!

In French, in most all cases, the final consonant sound of words is not pronounced. *Froid* is froi, *pain* is pa, *chaud* is chau. But hold on -- sometimes the sound of as many as *3, 4* even *5* letters -- both vowels and consonants, glued to the end of a word, will be dropped. *Au revoir les lettres!* THIS IS EARTH SHATTERING NEWS. This is why I believe French is the easiest romance language to learn.

This 'letter dump' will be your new best friend. It's the very reason that I decided to rebel against the French verb charts. (Coming next, in # 2)

Again, every one of the above ER verbs sounds the same. The E, ES, and ENT sounds of all endings are dropped. You could talk to, or refer to, seven different people, or groups, or things, and use the same sound.

This is our lovely, tight-knit, happily-ever-after family of seven, the famous Kumbaya clan. *Je, tu, il, elle, on, ils, elles* are the Kumbayas. (Yep, Kumbaya is their name. Right, it was a hippie chant in the 60's, and according to the Urban dictionary it still means "chill, unity." And that they are.)

In other romance languages the letters used on all verb endings, in fact everywhere, are *all* pronounced. There are no clumps of letters stuck on the end of any words that are not pronounced. Not a letter dump to be found. If a letter is there, in Italian, Spanish, Portuguese, etc., IT IS PRONOUNCED. So, *every* word must be memorized exactly as it's written. Brain power needed. No short cuts. Which means way more work for you.

On our verbs above, the E, ES and ENT sounds were all dropped, on every list. We have just ONE sound for each verb listed. PARL, MANG, and AIM. As we don't have to learn different sounds for every verb ending, for the seven personal pronouns, that makes seven times less work in French.

Wait – it gets better. The ER ending verbs make up over 80% of all French verbs. 80%! There are over 1,000 verbs with ER endings. *That's practically the whole French language*! Except for having to get to know a few major bad boys like *ÊTRE, AVOIR* and *ALLER* – you could probably live your entire life speaking only ER verbs and do just fine. (In *réalité,* there are over 12,000 French verbs, as listed in the Bescherelle verb book.)

And speaking of *ALLER*, this bad boy is the only one out of the 1,000 ER verbs that's irregular. Hold on… ONE irregular verb out of 1,000? Just ONE?

ALLER (to go) is one of the *baddest* bad boys of all the bad boys. He's defying all other ER verbs just to do his own thing. I'd introduce you now, but as usual *aller* had *to go.* He's off riding his Harley.

Why are those guys in wigs chasing me through the streets?

We're at point #2.

Here's where Coco leads those 17th century Academy members, dressed in silk culottes, charging down the Champs-Élysées brandishing bayonets and verb-filled parchment manuscripts. We're back at the changing of the guard, I mean, the changing of the guarded conjugation charts.

Now that we're clear on point #1 (many endings, one sound) it will be easy to see why it's time to tweak the good ol' verb charts.

First, take a look at this ridiculous *PARLER* chart below. Really? How could some nutty Academy member think that this silly chart would be...

Sorry, I meant to say: "Please take a gander at this most esteemed, *PARLER* verb chart as created by the illustrious French Academy. It was designed, as it is so preserved today, to maintain the purity and the...

Sorry, I got carried away. Where was I? Oh, yes, verb charts.

First, we're wheeling all of the ER verbs into the ER and amputating all endings. As you know, this is a surgery we'll be doing with all verbs: ER, IR, and RE endings. Verbs are all about the endings. The endings will tell you everything!

Here's the present tense, **PARLER**. The **ER** is chopped off the end, we've got the root, **PARL**, and we've added new endings needed to communicate with each person or group.

PARLER: To talk, to speak

Je parle

Tu parles

Il, elle, on parle

Nous parlons

Vous parlez

Ils, elles parlent

Wait! Look at that chart! Do you see anything odd? Do you see the problem? It's out of order! OUT. OF. ORDER.

For learning to speak French the easiest, fastest way possible, this chart is upside down. Totally wrong.

Remember what we saw in #1, the *letter dump*, where you don't pronounce the E, ES and ENT on the end of the ER verbs? And that those verbs make up over 80% of all present tense verbs? *That's over 1,000 verbs.* Shouldn't those verbs be kept together? Logical. But look at the chart.

There we were, going along nicely, right down the list with our lovely Kumbaya family that ALL sounds the same -- when BOOM! – someone throws a *NOUS* and *VOUS* right in the middle. These two jump in with all new sounds to learn. New endings. New pronunciation. What were they thinking? There are our poor kids, *ils* and *elles* abandoned, left alone, discarded at the bottom of the chart. This was a dastardly attempt to break up our cohesive little family. Kumbaya! Kumbaya! Kumbaya!

This is exactly what bugged me when I grabbed that two dollar book out of the library reject bin. Anyone can see that this chart is "off," can't they?

With one karate chop, we can change the whole list to help us learn French. And don't get me started but the *VOUS* and *NOUS* need some slapping around too. *Nous* we'll be sending to the gallows.

Do you realize what this all means? Not only will you save the time of learning 1000 *NOUS* conjugations everywhere, (you'll see) but you'll be one of the few rebels in the world to have the first new verb conjugation charts done in 384 years. This is staggering news. It's *la crème de la crème. La vie en rose. Le café au lait.*

Next there's a sneak peek at the new charts using our same three present tense verbs that we went over last chapter. *Parler. Manger. Aimer.* Our Kumbaya family of seven similar sounds is back together again. The ***vous*** was dropped down, out of the way. And the *nous* was -- hey, where is the ***nous***? It's in a tiny font at the bottom where it belongs. *Nous* is rarely used as "we" in spoken French today, instead it's ***ON, ON, ON*** all the way. True. *Nous* has been kicked out of spoken French. You'll see it used in writing, but basically you'll rarely hear the word *nous* spoken anymore. We'll get back to this in a bit.

These newly organized lists show how clean, neat, and simple French verb charts can be. And remember, these ER verbs make up 80% of all French verbs. Over 1,000 of these buggers. So yes, *this is a super big deal.* You can easily learn over 1,000 clean, neat, and simple ER verbs in the present tense *if* put in this new world order. Simply remove the ER from the end of the ER verbs, and add the **E, ES, E, ENT, EZ** ending, and presto -- you've conjugated most ER verbs in the present tense. (Which we've learned – is all but ONE ER verb.) And when you start our speaking a new language, you'll be using the present tense most of the time as you learn. You can communicate very well that way, too. People will still understand you.

PARLER (To speak/to talk)	**PRONOUNCED**
Je parl**e**	PARL
Tu parl**es**	PARL
Il parl**e**	PARL
Elle parl**e**	PARL
On parl**e**	PARL
Ils parl**ent**	PARL
Elles parl**ent**	PARL
Vous parl**ez**	PARL-A
Nous parl**ons**	PARLON

MANGER (To eat)	**PRONOUNCED**
Je mang**e**	MANJ
Tu mang**es**	MANJ
Il mang**e**	MANJ
Elle mang**e**	MANJ
On mang**e**	MANJ
Ils mang**ent**	MANJ
Elles mang**ent**	MANJ
Vous mang**ez**	MANJ-A
Nous mang**eons**	MANJON

AIMER(To love/like)	**PRONOUNCED**
J'aime	EM
Tu aim**es**	EM
Il aime	EM
Elle aime	EM
On aime	EM
Ils aim**ent**	EM
Elles aim**ent**	EM
Vous aim**ez**	EM-A
Nous aim**ons**	EMON

Adieu nous.

I know, I know, it's shocking to see *NOUS* disappearing. But trust me, in *spoken* French, *nous* is disappearing faster than mosquitoes in a hurricane. In fact – I'm taking *nous* off the chart completely. Not even leaving it in a tiny font at the bottom of the charts. This is all about learning to *parler,* to speak as quickly as possible, so *adieu nous.*

Here's how *NOUS* has morphed into *ON* today, and I'm sure you've said these exact things yourself:

ON mange avec Le Prince William, comme d'habitude chaque vendredi. (**WE** eat with Prince William, as usual, every Thursday.)

Comme d'habitude, ON a dit non, à George Clooney. (As always, **WE** said no to George Clooney.)

Oui, ON parle avec Brad Pitt *tous les jours, quand il appelle.* (Yes, **WE** speak to Brad Pitt every day, when he calls.)

Not a *NOUS* in sight. It's *ON. ON. ON.*

On is a master at playing double agent too; he's 007 and James Bond rolled into *one* as ON means both ONE.... and WE. Used as ONE we'd say: "Where does *one* enter the restaurant?" Or, "How would *one* really know the truth?" But even its use as *ONE* is becoming *passé,* outdated. As in English

23

today, *one* tends not to speak about *one*, unless *one* is teaching *one's* French literature class at *one's* favorite university, the Sorbonne. So *on* in French is mostly used as WE.

If you look at the three previous verb charts, *ON* is conjugated just like its brother and sister, *il* and *elle*. It's one of our seven member Kumbaya family of silent endings. (This is getting better all the time.) You still need to know *nous* exists and how to use it, but is it necessary to memorize it 1000 times, with every single *nous* pronoun; for every single verb, in every single tense? NO! Dagnabbit it, no! That's right, I said NO! (I'm on a roll. I think my meds are wearing off, or my gluten index is up, or my triglyceride levels are spiking. Grammar does that to me.)

TIP: The S in *nous* and *vous* is NEVER pronounced. NEVER! They're pronounced NEW and VEW... ALWAYS. While the sound of the consonant at the end of almost *every word* in French is dropped, the only time you'll hear *anything* at the end of *nous* (new) or *vous* (vew) is a **Z** sound, when they're doing a liaison with the next vowel. *Nou**Z** allons demain.* (We go tomorrow.) *Vou**Z** allez après-demain.* (You go the day after tomorrow). Is it *just* a liaison, or is it a dance between a shy wallflower vowel and its stronger consonant partner who jumped in to help? We'll see.)

I feel a spell coming on.

As the endings of the 1000 present tense ER verbs are never heard, you can easily forget how the endings are *written*. And once you add in all the other verbs you'll learn, like the IRs and REs, plus the bad boys, all in various tenses, it'll be easy to forget how to spell these silent ER endings. Here's a phrase I use to help me: IT'S EZ AND ESSENTIAL TO ENTERTAIN ME. I'll show you what it means, but remember -- I'm either a genius, or nuts, so if this doesn't help you, ignore it. Here's how it breaks down...

TU (informal you) refers to a buddy, dog, cat, teammate. *TU* is your friend and is **ESSENTIAL** in your life. These *TU* forms will always have an **ES** attached to the end of all ER present tense written French, like the **ES** starting **es**sential. *Tu manges, tu aimes, tu parles.*

(While *tu* verbs have an have ES ending in the present tense of all ER verbs -- *Tu in all tenses*, from the past to the future, in all verbs types ER, IR, RE *is major buddy-buddy* with the letter **S**. If there's a verb being conjugated for *tu* there's sure to be an **S** hanging around. Since the **S** will almost always be silent, it's easy to forget how to spell a *tu* verb. When in doubt, add an **S**, and you'll probably be right. (*Tu parles, tu parlais, tu parleras*.) When writing, I refer to *tu* as Stu, so I never forget he's probably got an S with him. Got that? Almost everywhere *TU* (or STU) has an S hanging around after conjugations -- in present tense tu has an ES.

ILS and *ELLES* are the most fun of the Kumbaya family group because they're plural. They're a couple, a bunch, or a crowd of people, animals, whatever, all hanging out. These are the ones that **ENTERTAIN**. You add an **ENT** to all of these endings. *Ils parlent, elles mangent, ils aiment.*

VOUS has been tossed down the chart to the bottom. It stands out, so it's **EZ** to remember. *Vous mangez, vous parlez, vous aimez.*

What about the rest of the gang: *je, il, elle, and* the double agent *on*? *Je* takes the lead here. Whatever *je* does in the present, *il, elle*, and *on* follow along. *Je* must be thinking that all these people are just like **ME**! And **ME** has just an **E** at the end. So does *Je parle, il aime, elle mange, on parle*. This is *Je* and her *ME* group.

Here's the big picture, the phrase: *It's easy and essential to entertain me*. It's **EZ** and **ES**sential to **ENT**ertain m**E**

Yes I know, you can't possibly think of all this while trying to speak – but you'll never need this when speaking, just when writing. **Donc**, if you're taking a test, or writing a review of this book (*merci*) or whatever you're doing, write that phrase in the margin. Then hopefully you can remember what the heck it means. Works for me. It's **EZ** and **ESSENTIAL** to **ENTERTAIN ME**.

Of the 50 verbs in 4.5 tenses that we'll study, which are the best ER verbs to learn first? We've already got *parler, manger,* and *aimer*. Let's add more. If you're an intermediate, of course you know all these basic words, but there are 1,000 more advanced, present tense regular ER verbs that you can plug into the chart below. This way, you can learn *any* in one minute! *C'est carrément facile.* (It's soooo easy).

Here's our new template for your own verb plug-ins. Notice I've put *il, elle, on* back together on the same line. *Ils* and *elles* are also side-by-side, just as they're found on most classic verb charts. (For centuries, thanks French Academy.) Grouping them together makes it easier as they conjugate the same, will be spelled with the same endings, and they'll take up less space in our cluttered minds.

Save this template for your special notebook. You do have a special notebook, right? Maybe I have a fetish, but I like to start out projects with a cool new notebook. You'll need one, too. Pick out a notebook, *queue tu aimes,* (that you love), and copy this verb template, you'll be using it a lot. Plus you'll need the notebook to write down expressions, links, word sets, and for conjugation and vocabulary help. Conjugation? Vocabulary? Yikes, grammar! Sounds super boring. But don't stress, it won't be. Remember, no one hates studying grammar more than me.

Your new notebook, *que tu aimes,* will be soon be filled with superheroes posing as bad boys, a double agent, wallflowers, and the famous Kumbaya family.

Here's our simple, amazing, magical, new template:

Je

Tu

Il, elle, on

Ils, elles

Vous

Let's get back to studying ER verbs…

Wait! Studying verbs? Nobody wants to study verbs.

Exactly, so kill the alert switch. Full steam ahead -- because there's nothing much to study. Remember, *French is friendly.*

Almost *everything*, in every chart below, will be spoken exactly the same way. Everything repeats over and over, and over. Just clean, neat, easy-to-learn verb sounds. BOOM.

But what about the rest from this upcoming list of regular ER verbs?

All the same. Just learn the verbs meanings (*donner*, to give; *rester*, to rest; *trouver,* to find, etc.) drop the ER at the end of the word -- and you've got the sound you need for all the personal pronouns, from *je* down the list to ***elles***. *Voilà*, you've just learned all present form spoken conjugations, for our entire ER list, in minutes.

By the way, vowels are the trick to good French pronunciation. Vowels, and the slightly difficult French R sound is where some English speakers have problems. Repeat these typical vowels sounds in English. Pronounce out loud: A. E. I. O. U.

If you can learn the correct French pronunciation of just these five letters, you can see a word and know pretty much how to say it correctly. (These same vowels sounds are applicable in many Latin based languages.)

Practice these French vowels sounds:

A = AHH (Like **Ahh**, this warm water feels great.)

E = EH (Like the **eh** of the slang word **meh**.. Did you like the concert? **Meh**.)

I = EEE (Like the English vowel E. **E**grets are happy birds.)

O = OHHH (Like English vowel O. **Ohh**, what a pretty Alpaca.)

U = EWW (Kinda like **Eww**, that fish is rotten!)

Listen to the vowels online to get a better grip on them in case my explanation above confuses you.

Once you get those French sounds down, keep repeating them as a set A.E.I.O.U., over and over till they become natural. They will and quickly.

27

Where were we? Verbs. Right, here are some more very useful verbs to add to your notebook, *que tu aimes*.

Remember, with *vous* we're using the good old American A sound as spoken in HAY, SAY, WAY, PAY, that big strong "A". For the following, you'll need that big fat A with all the *VOUS* verbs, as we are dropping the EZ sound completely and using just the English A sound on the end.

DEMANDER (To ask)	**PRONOUNCED**
Je demande	DEMAND
Tu demandes	DEMAND
Il, elle, on demande	DEMAND
Ils, elles demandent	DEMAND
Vous demandez	DEMAND-A

DONNER (To give)	
Je donne	DONN
Tu donnes	DONN
Il, elle, on donne	DONN
Ils, elles donnent	DONN
Vous donnez	DONN-A

TRAVAILLER (To work)	
Je travaille	TRAVAILL
Tu travailles	TRAVAILL
Il, elle, on travaille	TRAVAILL
Ils, elles travaillent	TRAVAILL
Vous travaillez	TRAVAILL-A

PENSER (To think)	
Je pense	PENS
Tu penses	PENS
Il, elle, on pense	PENS
Ils, elles pensent	PENS
Vous pensez	PENS-A

RESTER (To stay)	
Je reste	REST
Tu restes	REST
Il, elle, on reste	REST
Ils, elles restent	REST
Vous restez	REST-A

TROUVER (To find)	
Je trouve	TROUV
Tu trouves	TROUV
Il, elle, on trouve	TROUV
Ils, elles trouvent	TROUV
Vous trouvez	TROUV-A

HABITER (To live)	
J'habite	ABIT
Tu habites	ABIT
Il, elle, on habite	ABIT
Ils, elles habitent	ABIT
Vous habitez	ABIT-A

TIP: Note the *J'habite* above. The **H** is ALWAYS silent in French. *Habite* is abite. I've heard people struggle with this, trying to use a hushed H sound. Ignore the H completely when speaking, which makes the pronunciation even sharper and crisper. *Hotel* is simply OTEL. *Homme* is OMME. *Horrible* is ORRIBLE. Dump the H. (Sorry H).

FYI: in writing, the H can be contracted, or not contracted, as there are two types of H's. The contracted H *muet*, like *L'HOMME*, which acts like a vowel, and the uncontracted H *aspiré*, like *LE* HASARD which acts as a consonant. Both H's are not pronounced so you might want to forget everything I've just said and not confuse yourself. So just never pronounce any H, anywhere.)

The H is most often considered to be a vowel in French. I see vowels as wallflowers desperately needing help from the strong, flamboyant consonants around them. So help a poor vowel out. Whenever you see a weak vowel sound following another vowel make sure there's a consonant or apostrophe to jump in and help. For example in French there are 3 ways of writing the article THE: There's Le, La. L'. They already accounted for having to remove the E and A from LE and LA and given the L' its very own category. (If that doesn't make sense, it will later).

It's just like English, it doesn't sound right to hear *a eagle, a apple, a egg.* We quickly throw the powerful N to save the day. An eagle, an apple, an egg. Same in French, rely on the consonant in there to help the little ole vowels. (Je aime becomes J'aime, the J has shoved the E out of the way and an apostrophe rushed in to assist the weak A, stuck alone, starting out the word. Apostrophes have the same affect always able to help weak vowel sounds. *Que il sait*, will become *Qu'il sait*. (What he knows.)

Apostrophes are interesting characters in all languages. When an apostrophe shows up, it usually means that a letter was kicked out. It's there to show us something's missing.

The word o'clock, in old English started as *of the clock*. When clocks were still rare, people often told time by the sun too. To distinguish where the time was coming from, a clock, or the sun, people reporting the hour might say "it's two of the sun," or "two of the clock." In this case a letter and a whole word was dropped and it became o'clock. Do not = don't. Would not = wouldn't. It is = it's. Of course, you know all that, we've dropped letters everywhere and replaced them with a simple '. In French it's the same. Watch for apostrophes in French writings, get familiar with them. If you see one in a word, think about why it's there, what is the function? This will help you on your road to getting comfortable with French.

Contraction rules in French are stricter than in English. They're mandatory. In English we can say I am or say I'm. I have or I've. You would or you'd. We're easy going about it. But not the French. *J'ecoute* is never *je ecoute*. No choice. And watch out for vowels that may need help, they're hiding everywhere. Like *jusque ici* will become *jusqu'ici, lorsque on,* is written *lorsqu'on,* and *il se appelle* is always *il s'appelle.*

I don't want to go off into contraction-land, but note these mini words. These nine single consonants words love to contract: *Me, je, de, ce, le, ne, que, se.* All end with an E. This is a good learning game to play in a book or magazine written in French. Go through the text and pick out all the contractions using these nine tiny words. You'll be amazed at how often they show up and for how many different uses. *Tu* is not on the list. The U is very strong sounding and usually doesn't need any help.

Let's add more ER verbs to your list. Fill up your French language with tons of these easy to learn tenses. Grab all the ER's you can carry. They're the largest verb group, the most commonly used, and the easiest to learn – by far. Stock up on ER verbs. You can slay it in French with an army of easy to acquire ER verbs.

Remember, just remove the ER, and whatever's left, that's the stem, root (also called the *radical)*. What's left is the whole, exact, entire precise sound you need – it's all right there to correctly pronounce the entire family from *JE* to *ELLES*. Job done for you. (It's mind boggling, that the root word is ALL you need to speak to so many different people. What a gift.)

And here's another gift -- if you're just delving into the world of foreign languages, most learners -- that's millions of people -- start out speaking mostly in the present tense, as I've mentioned.

If you're traveling, or need to communicate right away, it's fine to speak in the present. You'll absolutely be understood. I start all my languages that way. I pick up all the basics and since the present tense is the most used, and most heard, it's easy to pick it up first. How else can you get your footing and learn? Don't expect to know all tenses before you speak. Jump right out using the present tense, it's extra valuable for new learners.

But stay calm. I'm throwing lots of info at you in this book. Don't worry. I'm trying to familiarize you with as much of the language as I can. You're not expected to learn everything to communicate. Pick up what you need now, and save the rest for reference to incorporate in the future, little-by-little. This book and your notebook, *que tu aimes,* will be waiting for you when you're ready to advance. Go at your own pace.

Here are more daily use verbs ready to have their ERs chopped off. And I hate to repeat myself, but this is sooooo amazing: Once that pesky ER is chopped off of any ER verb – the remainder is exactly all you need to speak correctly in the present tense, to 7 different people -- the entire Kumbaya clan. THE WORK IS DONE FOR YOU! It's so crazy. So simple. Such a gift! Wowza. Did you ever think you could *easily* speak in French? It truly is a friendly language.

INFINITIVE, ER VERBS	PRONOUNCED	
	KUMBAYA 7	VOUS
CHANGER (To change)	CHANG	CHANG-A
ÉCOUTER (To listen)	ECOUT	ÉCOUT-A
CHERCHER (To look for)	CHERCH	CHERCH-A
VISITER (To visit)	VISIT	VISIT-A
JOUER (To play)	JOU	JOU-A
SIGNER (To sign)	SIGN	SIGN-A
PASSER (To pass)	PASS	PASS-A
FABRIQUER (To make)	FABRIQ	FABRIQ-A
PRÉFÉRER (To prefer)	PRÉFÉR	PRÉFÉR-A
SEMBLER (To seem)	SEMBL	SEMBL-A
VOLER (To fly)	VOL	VOL-A
NAGER (To swim)	NAG	NAG-A
GOUTER (To taste)	GOUT	GOUT-A
FERMER (To close)	FERM	FERM-A
ACHETER (To buy)	ACHET	ACHET-A
LAVER (To wash)	LAV	LAV-A

(Laver can be reflexive if you're washing yourself, *je me lav*. (I wash myself). Above it's not used as a reflective verb so it would describe washing your car, the dishes, your dog, washing anything but yourself. Below *se laver* is now in the reflexive.

SE LAVER (To wash yourself)

I know – as discussed before, never compare your native language to your target language. But hey, I have, on occasion, rare occasion, (okay, not so rare) thought about French as compared to English. I've always thought re-

32

flexive verbs sounded weird in French: *Je me lav. Tu t'habilles. Il se lave.*
Tarzan talk. You Jane, me Tarzan. I me wash. You, you dress. He, he wash-
es. Meanwhile, we're using the same weird reflexive in English: "I'm gonna
sit myself down here for a bit." Or, "I'm gonna *make myself* some eggs." Or,
"I'll *take myself* a shower later." We do the same things in our own language.

Now it gets interesting. We have to know these verbs inside and out. We all
know the best way to learn a language is immersion in a foreign country.
Move to France, Morocco, Martinique, or any French speaking land -- fall
madly in love with a local *romantique*, stay with this significant other for a
year, and you'll not only speak French, you'll probably make *crème brûlée*.

But what if you're in Mosier, Oregon? Pensacola, Florida? Chandler, Arizona? How do you practice and use French all day? If a month at the Carlton
Hotel, Cannes, is off radar, let's do the next best thing. Let's bring France to
you. It's easy and fun. With just a little creativity you can tote France around
with you all day long.

Pump up your vocabulary as we go.

First, to play around with the verbs, let's take a look at the vocabulary, the
supporting cast you'll build around them. How much French vocabulary do
you know? A few words? Tons? If you're a super beginner, collect words.
Write them in that special notebook, *que tu aimes*. (There's the **ES** on *aimes*,
from it's **EZ** and **ES**SENTIAL to **EN**TERTAIN ME. Or Stu is back -- the
omnipresent S with TU.)

If you use certain words or expressions often in English, get the French
equivalent. Don't just grab basic words, like colors, days of the week, or
weather conditions. Collect whole expressions.

TIP: While studying vocabulary, always remember: *a lone word, like a lone
wolf*, is in dangerous territory.

When learning languages, it's never smart to learn a lone word (lone wolf)
without at least an article attached. You shouldn't learn *bateau, verre, che-
mise, chien*. (boat, glass, shirt, dog). You're not a dictionary. You don't need
to memorize thousands of unrelated words. Nobody has ever had an intelli

gent, memorable conversation with a dictionary. (Okay, but I was drinking tequila.)

The more information you can attach to the word, the better. You might learn *le verre, le bateau, une table, les chiens*. This additional information assures that you automatically connect the gender and/or number attached to the word. You have a *word set*. Make all your words clingy, like sticky rice. But sorry, that's not good enough. Nope. Not here. You need to absorb whole expressions, sentences, phrases.

Let's go further, add more information. You should always have enough vocabulary to fill out sentences, or keep enough vocabulary in your notebook to refer to. Grab an item, like *le verre* (the glass) and some colors: *bleu, orange, vert, or gris*. Now you have *le verre bleu*. Grab a list of sizes to pull from: *petit, grand, lourd, léger*. Now you have *le petit verre bleu*. Is the glass full, empty, broken? How about empty? Now it can be *le petit verre bleu vide*. Where is the glass? Use another word you're learning, like table. Now you have *le petit verre bleu vide sur la table*.

Don't just SAY the words, SEE the image. Imagine *le petit verre bleu vide sur la table*. Better yet -- put a real *petit verre bleu vide sur la table*. Grab *le verre bleu*, or *le verre rouge*, or *le verre clair*, and use it. Put it *sur la table*. Put it on the counter. In the hall. Put it next to the lamp beside your bed. With this one prop you can learn through dozens of new scenarios playing with *le verre bleu*. Trade the glass in for a tiny match box car, a red gummy bear... Take the item with you. (Yes, I'm serious!) Apply all the word sets and sentences you have. That's how you learned when you were five years old. Five. Immersion. Spending time IN the language every day.

Learn your favorite expressions. Do you always say: "Wow, that's crazy?" (*Wow, c'est fou!*) Or, "whatever!"? (*Peu importe!*) Or "too bad?" (*Tant pis* or *dommage*). Learn the French *équivalents*. Words, phrases, descriptions, everything that makes up your world in English, will become your world in French. Your language is your world. (Like Camus said: "The French language is my homeland.") So dear traveler, collect lots of descriptive words and expressions – write them in your notebook, we'll be needing them to bring France to you.

Memory tip: Label items in your house with their French names. From the fridge to the faucet. The computer to the chair. Label. Label. Label. You'll see the correct word around you all day. Label in *word sets*. (We're dealing with sticky rice.) Your couch could be labeled: My big red couch. (*Mon gran canapé rouge*). The fridge is cold. (*Le frigo est froid*). My little bedside clock. (*Ma petite horloge de chevet*.)

Make sure you know the correct pronunciation. Check online, try wordreference.com, Google translate, Rhinospike, Reverso. Lots of great apps are available. Get the exact pronunciation of the words. Memorize the word as spoken, *not* as written especially with the letter dumps in French. (As we know, *parlent* is pronounced *parl*. If you were to say *parlent*, few people might know what you mean.) Read these labels out loud. Talk to yourself. Use the words as often as possible. Your mind will automatically absorb the words. You won't realize how quickly it's happening, but it is. Trust the process.

Remember, you'd never like to see a lone wolf out struggling to survive. A lone word, too, is in a dangerous territory.

Opposites Attract.

Here's a way to get around new languages when you still have limited vocabulary – speak in opposites. Yep. If you only know how to say *tall* in a language -- you can express short too. If you only know how to say *thin* you can express the word *fat* too. (For some reason I have a block against the word **forgot** in Portuguese. A simple, basic word, but I can never remember it. I always say **I don't remember**, instead. Works perfectly.)

This simple trick you can always use. Let's say I'm at a police station with Officer *Mercibien*. I'm describing a bandito who just stole my new Chanel bag. Using the few words I know I can still communicate. I might say, "I don't remember." (I don't know how to say I forgot.) "He's not tall." (I don't know how to say short). "He does not have blonde hair." (I don't know how to say brown hair). "He is not thin." (I don't know how to say fat.) You get the idea.

Say the opposite, use the words you know. People will fill in the blanks for you.

When I tell Officer *Mercibien* above that the bandito is not short, not thin and doesn't have blonde hair -- bet he'll say "Okay, so he's tall, fat, and has brown hair? And was it a real Chanel bag, or a fake?" The words you need will usually be handed to you. *C'est parfait!*

If you're already a vocabulary wizard, perfect, then it's even easier to bring France transatlantic. You'll need lots of random *word sets* in your new creative French endeavors.

And while we're talking about vocabulary, here's a trick to learn over ONE HUNDRED new French words in ONE miniute. Nope, that's not a typo. You might already know this, but even if you do, this little trick is underused by us all. It's about zoning in on word endings. There are hundreds of words at your beck-and-call if you focus on word endings. (Yes, as grammar nerds know – I mean *suffixes*.)

The first time I was in Brazil I spoke no Portuguese. On the way from the airport into Rio, I saw a road sign that taught me my first 100 words. The large metal sign showed a man wearing a hard hat, and holding a shovel. Above him were two words: ATTENÇÃO CONSTRUÇÃO.

Hmm. Attention. Construction. Ah ha, then *TION* endings in English were simply changed to a *ÇÃO* ending in Portuguese. I couldn't yet say "hello" but I could say projection, radicalization, supposition, determination, even institutionalization in Portuguese. I suddenly knew maybe one hundred advanced words.

While most language learners know about these suffix changes, I don't think we use them enough. These are all easy-to-grab, advanced words *that we've already learned.*

Here are just a few of the many endings to watch for and examples of the endless words you can glean from them; new word endings you can add to the notebook, *que tu aimes.*

ENGLISH	FRENCH

TION =   **TION**
Emotion   Émotion
Evaluation   Evaluation
Detention   Détention

OUS =   **EUX**
Prestigious Prestigieux
Industrious Industrieux
Dangerous   Dangereux

LY =   **MENT**
Evidently   Évidemment
Rapidly   Rapidement
Apparently Apparemment

ORY =   **OIRE**
Glory   Gloire
Memory   Memoire
Laboratory Laboratoire

ARY =   **AIRE**
Military   Militaire
Extraordinary Extraordinaire
Argumentary   Argumentaire

IC =   **IQUE**
Authentic   Authentique
Fantastic   Fantastique
Intergalatic Intergalactique

ISM =   **ISME**
Existentialism Existentialisme
Journalism   Journalisme
Exceptionalism Exceptionnalisme

Imagine… there you are at *le Louvre*, admiring a Dutch masterpiece, you *barely* speak a word of French but you can whisper to the stranger beside you as she eyes the painting, and be 100% correct to say, in advanced French…

"*Évidemment, c'est manifique, fantastique, extraordinaire. C'est exception-nalisme, non?*"

"Oh, you're French. Sorry, I don't speak *français.*" she says.

Tee-hee.

There are lots of big, useful, powerful words that you've spent a lifetime learning in English that will usher your French into the big leagues with very little effort. Don't leave home without them.

ATTENÇÃO: Sometimes when doing a quick change on a suffix, other little changes will occur within the word. Above you'll see some double letters appear, like "apparently" becomes *apparemment*, and other small changes, but you'll be 90% there, and usually 100% there. Often the word sounds the same anyway so don't get too hung up.

Okay, we've got some of the vocabulary situation down. We're collecting new words daily. We're using real French expressions. Our fridge is labeled. We've got the list of great ER verbs and their silent endings. We're getting there. *Petit à petit* we're advancing. But first…

Introducing the missing links.

You can quickly accelerate your vocabulary learning even more, and sound *really* French, when you add a bit more sticky rice to your sentences. These powerful word bridges next will add a touch of bling to your speech and help accessorize your *français.*

Don't stress here. You don't have to memorize this list. Pick out a few of these links and expressions and sprinkle them around in your day. Just three or four for now. Between the suffixes we just looked at and these links don't bog yourself down. Don't burn yourself out. Keep it fun.

Grab a few links words here and try them out. Say them out loud. (Some of the links I lean on are: e*t alors, de toute façon, donc, parce que, mais oui, c'est ça,* and *de temps en temps.*) Once you get very buddy-buddy with them, choose a few new ones, little-by-little get to know them, use them.

D'abord	First
Tout d'abord	First of all
Avant tout	Before anything
Premièrement	First of all
En premier lieu	In the first place
Mais	But
Cependant	However
Pourtant	However
En fait	In fact
En réalité	In reality
Avec	With
Beaucoup	Many/a lot
À vrai dire	To tell the truth
Autrement dit	In other words
En un mot	In a word
Tout de même	All the same
Quand même	As well
Au fait	By the way
A ce sujet	On this subject
Toujours	Always
Justement	Exactly
Des temps en temps	From time to time, sometimes
Comment no	Of course
Bien sûr	Of course
Ou... ou...	Either.... or
Ou bien	Or rather
En général	In general/generally
Grâce à	Thanks to
Et	And
Généralement	Generally
D'ailleurs	Anyway
Par exemple	For example
En tout cas	In any case
De toute façon	At any rate
Cela dit	That said

Ici	Here
Après tout	After all
En conclusion	In conclusion
Quand même	Still
Et voilà	There you go, there it is
En effet	Exactly
C'est ça	That's right
Et alors?	And?
Mais non!	But no!
Mais oui!	But yes!
Parce que / Car	Because
Donc	So
Puisque	Since
Comme	As/since
Lorsque/quand	When
Ensuite/puis	Then

Add a few links to your household labels, say them out loud. *Le frigo est froid* could be written: *Et voilà, le frigo est froid. (*Here it is, the fridge is cold.) *Ma petite horloge de chevet, est toujours ici. (*My little bedside clock is always here.) Sneak in as many words as you can. Read. Remember. Repeat.

Maybe you're thinking: Wait, *donc,* what does this have to do with the 4.5 tenses of the 1,000 ER verbs that make up 80% of the French language? And how do we bring France to us? Are you stalling?

Will the Eiffel Tower make it past airport security? *MAIS OUI!*

Remember that I mentioned pages ago that French would be learned in your imagination, by your own creative self? I meant it. We're bringing France to you. All day long. While you're returning that *petit t-shirt blanc* to Macys. (Small, white T-shirt.) While driving your *jeune gros chien* (fat, young dog) to the doggie park. While you *regardes le football rapide.* (Watch fast football.*)* Not a lone wolf here, all word sets.

All day you're interacting with people, places, and things. And these people, places, and things are going to teach you French. We'll enter this world soon. First let's grab the verbs, here's where the vocabulary joins them.

Whether you speak almost no French or can weave together sentences, we need to apply the words we've learned. Another no brainer, right? You'd be shocked how many people memorize new words, then don't use them. Rarely speak them out loud. Quickly forget them.

I used to think it was crazy when people said they were forgetting a language, *even their own native language.* I thought those hard-earned words were scorched into my mind. But after 20 years of not speaking Italian I could barely order a *penne arrabiata* in a Milan restaurant. Word-by-word my Italian had tiptoed off, deserted me, and snuck away for a dip in the Tivoli fountain. I hadn't even noticed.

Grab your new list of ER verbs. Now you'll not only learn more French, you'll develop your observation skills. After this training, you could be hired as a private eye. (A *private* eye? Yep, English is vivid.)

Welcome to Frenchville...

*B*ienvenue. Here you can speak to everyone you meet, all day long, in French.

"What?" you say. "*Sacre bleu*! In French? *Mais non*! *Pas possible!*

Calm down. Engage the people, places, and things all around you. Observe them. Tell yourself what you see. Yes, welcome to the imaginary world of Frenchville.

See the guy near you buying cigarettes in the Circle K? Tell yourself about him using the French vocabulary and ER verbs you're learning. Since you probably won't hear French spoken about town all day – generate it. Create the French world around you. Describe the people, places and things. Interact with them in your head. Think French. Make up scenarios. Humor yourself.

Take the little notebook, *que tu aimes,* out on a jaunt with you. Sit in your local coffee shop, or hangout and observe the people and items around you. Can you pull any words out of your head to describe them? He is fat. Coffee is cold. She is blonde. If not go through your notebook. Go down the list of new vocabulary and verbs and apply them, check them off as you go. The idea is to get comfortable using them, applying them. Make up sentences, scenarios, create a secret world, your own secret Frenchville.

Back to *l'homme* (Pronounced *l'omme*, right?) buying cigarettes from the lady at the Circle K register. If I were in Frenchville, I'd use as many verbs, links, expressions and vocabulary that I could pull from my memory or notebook. I'd make the sentences as simple, or as complex as I'd like. You might say to yourself...

Il parle avec elle. (He talks to her.) *Il achète des cigarettes.* (He buys the cigarettes) *C'est un homme.* (He's a man) *C'est une femme.* (She's a woman.)

Or you might get really ambitious and try as many words as possible, using expressions, vocabulary links, and conjugated verbs. (Hold on, you'll soon see that the following is a super simple sentence that YOU KNOW.)

De temps en temps, il achète des cigarettes, et il parle beaucoup avec elle. C'est fou!

Don't get nervous. That might look like WAY too much French; might look like gibberish to you. Let's break it down: It reads: From time-to-time he buys cigarettes and he talks to her a lot. It's crazy! *(De temps en temps, il achète des cigarettes, et il parle beaucoup avec elle. C'est fou!)*

Can you pick out what we've used there? That's 3 links, 2 ER verbs, 3 personal pronouns, 1 noun, and 2 of our new bling expressions. But more than that – it's a whole sentence, not a great one, but a whole one. You're thinking in sentences. *Mon Dieu!*

But wait, what about the magical suffixes? We've got another few hundred words to pull from. (I'm the one who said we don't use them enough and here I go forgetting them?) I'm gonna leave this up to you. Throw in your choice of big time French words, like maybe an *apparently*, or *evidently* or you can make her *extraordinary*, or make him *intergalactic*. Better yet, put him in *detention*. Or make him *dangerous*. These are all in your suffix list. Go ahead, you've got hundreds of your own KNOWN advanced words readily available.

Create your own sentences. These are super simple. Just to give you an idea: *Il achète des cigarettes parce qu'il aime les cigarettes.* (He buys cigarettes because he likes cigarettes.) *Ils aiment parler ensemble.* (They like to talk together.) *Elle aime cet homme? Mais non!* (She loves that man? No!). *Elle est jolie et elle aime parler avec cet homme.* (She is pretty and she likes to talk to that man.)

Don't sweat it if you didn't understand those sentences when written in French. They're just very simple constructions, a combination of the basic ER verbs we've learned in the present tense, plus a few expressions and links pulled from the previous list, all added to basic vocabulary words. But hey, you're dealing in complete thoughts already. *C'est cool*! (*Cool* is used a lot in France today, just like we do, meaning – cool, great, hip.)

It's possible to be a beginner and speak in full sentences, real sentences, that make sense. Once you write or say your creative sentences it can be a game to figure out what your recipe was. For the example above I wrote: *Il achète des cigarettes parce qu'il aime les cigarettes.* That's 2 ER present tense verbs, 2 personal pronouns, 2 articles, 1 link, and 1 noun. Have I missed anything? There's even a contraction: *que il = qu'il.* The E was dropped making it a faster, better sounding sentence. The word was rescued by the apostrophe to become *qu'il*. If you don't know why the *des* was used, think of it as "some" here. Google it. Hey, I can't explain everything right now.

Going out for a walk? What do the trees look like? The houses? Streets? Everything around you can be used. Whatever level you're at, use the words you're learning, no matter how simple or complex. The tree is big. The house is pretty. The street is long. As you learn the basics, add on more words. The tree is very big, it is near the house, and on a very long, wide street. The easiest way to memorize words is to connect them with visuals, like those items all around you.

It can be fun to use French books or magazines and break down the story. Hunt down your target verb, or word, or link. How many present tense ER verbs can you find per page? Or find all the places that *avoir* and *aller* are hiding in plain sight. Next time you're stuck in a waiting room, bring along a French article and go on the hunt for your chosen verb, or link, or expression. You'll learn a lot. (This is WORD SAFARI which we'll get into later. It's like grammar, only fun.)

44

Visit Frenchville as often as possible. Form sentences and apply them to the world around you. Practice. Keep yourself immersed in *français*. Think in French. Even if you only know a few words – use them. Like a five year old learning a language. They will keep using and repeating the words they know. *C'est fabuleux!*

Are you way more advanced? Use bigger word sets, assorted tenses, more progressive verbs. Plug these advanced ER verbs into the chart. Try *serrer, gêner, entraver, fouiller, soupirer, picoter.* Keep the conversation going. Using the words you've studied, repetition will carve an auto-route in your memory. Use the words. Use the words. Use the words. (Yep, I like to repeat myself.) Trust the process. Your mind will automatically work for you to learn these new words.

There are lots of other ways to bring France to you. Some might choose French classes. Maybe not the expensive Berlitz classes downtown, but Google local senior centers, (any age can go), libraries, parks, night classes at community colleges. Google local Meet Ups, these groups are in every city and have loads of get-togethers with native speakers and learners in every language.

Check out your local Craigslist under Community, find the interested language aficionados. Place your own free Craigslist post in Paris, Monaco, Brussels. Advertise worldwide that you're looking for a French speaker to exchange with. French people studying English worldwide would love to Skype with you. They're in the same boat navigating choppy grammar waters.

There are language lovers everywhere. Facebook groups abound. Plus you'll find free online videos teaching you *every aspect* of French language learning. There are apps you can use, like Preply or Fiverr, where you can find native language teachers worldwide, who charge as little as $4.00 an hour for online classes.

Singer Julio Iglesias taught me Spanish and French. Pop artist Lucio Dalla taught me Italian. Brazilian Singer Maria Bethânia taught me Portuguese.

You can ace languages by listening to music. Especially slower music, ballads, boleros, torch songs, love songs, or any well pronounced songs. I've always learned languages that way. For me it's been the most effortless, most beautiful way to learn. I loved the music of romance languages so much, it's the big reason I learned them – to understand the lyrics. Without a doubt music was my muse for acquiring *les langues.*

In my 20's I was working in a bar in Quito, Ecuador and spoke almost no Spanish. I had come from living in the Amazon for over a year and spoke only basic Huaorani, a remote jungle language. (Note to self: Learn practical languages. It's better if you don't have to maneuver a dugout canoe down a raging river teeming with anaconda, past a lake full of piranha, into a remote Indian village just to find someone else who speaks the language.)

Back to the bar in Quito. I would listen, in tears, as Julio Iglesias sang *El Amor* or *Abrazame.* (Cornball, I know, but hey these are ballads. Boo-hoo). I had no idea what he was singing but I learned every sentiment, memorized every song, even before I knew what the words meant. And slowly, effortlessly, I began to understand, and use the word sets I'd heard him sing.

I remember an Ecuadorian girl telling me, in broken English, that she'd just come from Miami, had to go to Guayaquil, then to Bogota. I blurted out *"de tanto correr por la vida sin frenos."* Wait, what? I could barely order fried eggs in Spanish. How did an entire advanced sentence pop out? It was the opening line of a song that was etched in my mind. It meant: *running around the world without brakes.* I had absorbed that and pulled it out at the right moment. Boom! Our minds are brilliant at putting puzzles together. Trust it.

Music. Portable, fun and engaging. You can customize it and listen to any genre, at any time. Music. It's more sticky rice for language learning; the lyrics of your favorite songs will cling to you forever. Bet you know songs you learned as a child. (Rudolf the Red Nosed Reindeer? Jingle Bells?)

Yes, music is my top choice for learning languages. It'll help you with pronunciation, vocabulary and you'll effortlessly learn whole phrases, useful expressions, not just single words. But bigger bonus yet – music is your personal invitation deep into the culture. Getting to know everyone from the yesterday's iconic singers (Jacques Brel, Édith Piaf, Yves Montand, Charles

Aznavour) to today's newest hit makers. Music will give you a leg up straight into the heart of the French culture (English again... *leg up.*)

Yes, Julio taught me Spanish. I had traveled the world listening to him; he was always there teaching me, accompanying me. When I moved to the *Cote d'Azur,* I bought his music in French, it was like taking a private tutor along, a familiar voice that I had heard every day for years.

(My good friend Abel Tabuyo later road managed Julio's career for 14 years before leaving to work for Enrique. What are the odds? I not only spent time with Julio, I had VIP treatment at countless shows, and years later sold Julio's red Testarosa, and worked on the sale of his Gulfstream jet. To spend time with him was one of life's rare full circle moments. It could never convey to him how much his music meant to me.)

Today the internet is all about worldwide music. I subscribe to I-Heart Radio. Along with the songs, the lyrics are shown in the language sung. Right now I'm trying to get my Italian back, pulling it out of the Tivoli Fountain. (Any Italians? I'm listening to classics from Mina, Gino Paoli, Lucio Dalla, and Ornella Vanoni).

There are great French radio stations online. Most will have occasional songs in English, much beloved by the French, but French law is that 40% of all broadcasts must be in French.

Don't worry if you can't understand much said on the radio, it's spoken at a naturally fast pace. Listen to the pronunciation, pick out word sets and repeat them, work on your accent. Mimic the D.J. And most of all absorb the French music.

Radio France, biggest French syndicate, news, music, interviews, all over France and worldwide.

FIP, underground gems, jazz, electronic, world music. Mostly female D.J.s, who must have "smooth, soft, mesmerizing voices" to be hired.

Radio Nova, Not a free channel, but has a 30-day free trial. Lots of interviews, podcasts, music. (I'm listening to Nova right now, there were a few commercials, then the DJ was rattling on in French, and now they're playing the Rolling Stone's: *Under My Thumb.*)

RFI, Radio France International, founded by the French government. A public broadcasting radio, with over 40 million listeners, it's one of the most iconic stations in the world.

News in Slow French, real news, happening right now - in varying speeds for beginners, intermediate and advanced levela.

France Inter Main Public Radio. *Emblematic* music, meaning iconic tunes.

France Culture, Podcasts and interviews with today's top newsmakers.

Rire et Chansons, Popular comedy radio. One comedy *emission, Les Grosse Têtes*, has been running daily for over 40 years.

Nostalgie, '70s and '80s classic songs in English and French. 68% of all music dates back from before the 2000s.

Chante France, Dedicated to only French *chansons*, beautiful music from all decades.

Lyrics are a *magnifique* way to learn languages. While I can't figure out the words to many American songs, I can follow along with the correct lyrics to *innumerable* foreign *chansons*. (People hear Elton John singing: *Hold me closer 'Tony Danza,'* when it's been *'tiny dancer.'*)

As mentioned before, I-Heart Radio has lyrics along with most songs, but there are lots of great apps and online sites to choose from.

Lyrics Training is a free, fun Google app that'll help you learn a bunch of languages including French.

Musixmatch is a great app, the world's largest collection of lyric connected to Spotify and I-Heart and it shows the lyrics to all the songs in both the original language, and English translation.

Podcasts are another sticky rice form of learning French. Like books, find subjects that fascinate you. (Yep, still diamond heists) and you'll learn a ton of new French *bons mots*.

I-Heart Radio has *News in Slow French* and assorted interesting podcasts. If you can't afford subscribing to *News in Slow French*, they broadcast the first

20 minutes of every podcast for free. Listening to slow French too often can be detrimental as no one speaks that slowly. (Except my Aunt Josephine.)

Daily French Pod, perfect for beginners, full of podcasts, keywords, grammar tutorials, vocabulary and a community of native speakers to practice with. (Most podcasts are entirely in French so if you're a true beginner, French Pod 101, next, might be better.)

French Pod 101, interesting, informative conversations followed by slow speed recordings translations and explanations about the culture. One of the top-rated French podcasts.

Coffee Break French, 15-minute lessons where French teacher, Mark, mentors a young French learner. (Mark is Scottish, his accent is *impeccable,* and having learned French as an adult, he understands the pitfalls of acquiring languages.)

One Thing in a French Day, we follow native speaker Laetitia through her daily life in France. She only speaks in French, but has transcripts available.

Le Journal en Français Facile, a daily podcast broadcasting the most important, most current news stories. Each episode comes with a free transcript.

Écoute Ç, a website where people show off their singing abilities, or inabilities. From top notch to low brow, it's fun exposure to French. (I just watched a Frenchman imitating Édith Piaf singing *La Vie en Rose* as he strummed his ukulele. Crazy.)

Keep listening to French. Don't listen to any podcasts that communicate with lots of English. Listen to French! Even if you don't understand all that's being said -- the more French the better. Listen. Listen. Listen. French. French. French. You're absorbing it all the time. Your mind is accepting the new words, the new accent, the new pronunciation. You may not realize it, but it's settling in with French. It's recognizing and accepting this new form of communication. The more exposure the better.

The brain works like a floating duck. The duck glides effortlessly across the lake. Not even a wake behind him. All smooth. But underneath, unseen, those yellow feet are paddling like crazy to keep him moving forward. While you may *believe* that you're casually listening to a French podcast, or some new pop *chanson*, your mind is paddling furiously underneath, grasping at words, grammar, intonation, pronunciation, grabbing parts and pieces, putting it all together to keep propelling you forward. Trust the process.

As PhD and language expert Paul Sulzberger noted after extensive research: "Neural brain tissue required to learn and understand a new language will develop *automatically* from simple repeated exposure to the language – which is how babies learn their first language."

SRS Flashcards. Although not music related, this is another fun interactive way to learn languages. SRS (Spaced Repetition System) is a form of memorizing data, vocabulary, using computer based flashcards. By your response to the flashcards, the software can estimate when to bring back each word, at various intervals, repetitively, as often as the program estimates that you need to see the word again.

Anki, is the Godfather of repetitive learning software. A free program, you can learn to memorize anything from the world's top languages, to the world's top breed of cats. There are over 80 million flashcards available and tens of thousands of subjects.

Other SRS programs: **Brainscape, Quizlet, Cram, Tiny Cards, Study Blue, Studystack,** and **Flashcards +.** Some are free, others have monthly subscriptions. (Quizlet was founded by American Andrew Sutherland when he was 15 yrs old who created it while studying for a French final. He now has over 300 million subscribers. Andrew is just 23. Speak of superheroes.)

Facebook is a great asset for language learning. FB has assorted pages where you can trade English classes with native French people, swapping them for French lessons. Search FB under French, language learning, and language exchange, among others.

For all you game players, (aren't we all?) there are amusing, free apps everywhere for gam-ifying your life. You can almost forget you're learning and just have fun. **Poly Lingual, Digital dialects, French-Games.net, Sporcle, Quia French**, etc. Most game apps can help you at any level, from beginner to advanced, and teach everything from easy phrases to difficult verbs. (Aren't all verbs difficult? Ugg, sorry, I just hate grammar.)

For the more advanced, Google **Trivia Quiz**, **French** and you'll find lots of word games in French. If you like hard copies, you can buy fun word games, like puzzle books and word searches. Right now I'm playing with *The Ultimate Portuguese Word Search Collection,* 200 pages full of puzzles to find words in. It's kinda fun if you're a language nerd.

There are also apps like **Memrise, Duolingo, Mondly and Busuu** where you earn points for continuing daily.

Oh là, là, on va au cinéma! As you know, Netflix is great for learning a language. You can change the language spoken, and the subtitles shown. Choose what's best for you. Watch in French with French subtitles, so you can see the words. Or French with English subtitles, to hear French and see the translation. (A great way to start out.) You might watch it various ways then re-watch it with NO subtitles in French to see how you do. (I always have my finger on the pause button when using subtitles to learn a language. I freeze everything to take a look at the words spinning by quickly. The pause button is your best friend when learning. Also, go to your TV's settings and enlarge the size of the subtitles, that's also helpful.)

There's every combination of ways to alter the language and subtitles to speed up your language learning. I rarely watch a film or TV series on Netflix without subtitles running in some language. Like music and games, it's a fun, engaging way to learn.

Don't forget your TV. I've got Sling TV and bought their French package for $15.00. I get talk shows, reality TV, episodic and movies straight from France. See what your cable or TV provider offers. There's also a kinda new app called

Lingopie and others that can translate words for you as you learn a language watching movies and TV. I haven't tried it but it looks interesting.

Talk to the TV. I'm serious. This is a fantastic way to communicate with real (fake) people. Have a conversation with the actors speaking on the show. Interject your link words from your notebook, too. Ask them questions. I know, sounds crazy, right? But it's super effective.

The actor might say in French on screen: "But where is Jean, where did he go?" Hit the remote's PAUSE button. You might answer in French "Jean is gone. He left yesterday." Or you might agree with him and just repeat what he says. Or phrase it as a question.

Keep your finger on the PAUSE button. Stop the TV so you have time to answer or time to repeat their words. For example, the actor yells in French, "She's crazy, she hung up the phone." Pause the TV. You might agree in French, repeating his words out loud: "Yes, she's crazy, she hung up the phone." Or maybe you'll disagree and say that's she's *not* crazy and did *not* hang up the phone. You'll be actively "interacting with someone" and learning the exact pronunciation of the words they used. It's like having a private tutor in your house. Rewind, relisten and answer. Remember, if you have subtitles on (you do, right?) you'll be able to SEE what they're saying too. It makes watching TV more active and not passive. Try it. It's fun, and silly, and educational, to talk back to the TV. The remote's pause button is your best friend.

One of the BEST APPS ever is **HelloTalk**. Over 30 million people exchanging languages, conversing for FREE worldwide. Pair up, ASAP.

Parlez vous français?

Engage in conversations with any French speakers you meet. Don't be shy. Hear someone speaking English with an accent? Here's my *go to* question: "Excuse me, where is your beautiful accent from?" (Otherwise they might feel you are insulting them by stating they are speaking poor English, with a notable accent.) If they're French speakers… jump in. Have something always ready to say, like: "*J'aime le français. C'est ma langue préférée.*" (I love French. It's my favorite language.

Hopefully they'll speak a little French with you. As a beginner, not knowing many words, it may be difficult, but try to stay in French. Use as much French as you can. They may want to switch back to English, but try to keep speaking French. They'll get the message that you're learning, and hopefully they'll help you out. (How's their English? Can you swap contact info and help each other by exchanging lessons?)

Since native languages speakers tend to race through words, try to slow them down with "Plus lentement, s'il vous plait." (Slower please.) Or "Je ne comprends pas." (I don't understand.) Have such a sentence always ready. If you speak slowly, that too has been shown to slow another speaker down.

And please note, many times I miss what is being said. We can easily misunderstand or don't know certain words. As all language pupils, we learn to pick out words we recognize and put the sentences together. It's normal. Then as you learn more, instead of knowing one or two words in the sentence, you may know five. Then six. Then one day the whole sentence. But it's hit and miss for everyone learning languages. WE'RE ALL FIGURING IT OUT. YOU ARE NOT ALONE. There are people worldwide doing the same thing. Welcome aboard. And remember -- when you're alone studying French you really aren't alone. There are millions of people, right along with you, all studying languages at that same moment. You're in good company. Great company.

Hold on. Back to grammar. What about those pesky IER endings?

What about those important, complicated IER verbs like *copier, crier, modifier, négocier, étudier, skier, simplifier, vérifier*, and all the others? Now what?

Nothin' to them. *They're just plain old ER verbs.* IER = ER. It's just the ER that's there to go into surgery. It doesn't matter if a verb ends in IER, (*skier*) or SER, (*penser*) or TER, (*écouter*) or VER, (*arriver*). It doesn't matter *what* comes before the mega important ER ending here. With IER verbs you're still just dropping the ER and leaving the **i** on the stem.

People handle **IER** verbs with kid gloves due to fears about conjugating. (Kid gloves? English again.) It's the **ii** syndrome. Double **ii**'s seem incorrect to English speakers but since we are removing the **ER** and leaving the **I** we can end up with certain conjugations, like the *imparfait,* with the ii syndrome. Like *vous copier = vous copiiez; Étudier = vous étudiiez; Skier = vous skiiez.* (Don't worry about the *imparfait.* It's easy and we'll get to it later.) Simply put, the **IER** gets no special treatment, it's just like any other friendly **ER** verb ending.

53

While *ALLER* is the only true, crazy, rebel ER irregular bad boy, a few ER verbs do have changes in spelling or accent marks when conjugated. But remember there are over 1,000 regular ER verbs so if a handful have minimal changes, that's a blip on our radar screen. 99% are good to go.

Verbs with these following endings will have small spelling changes: CER (*lancer*) GER (*manger*) ELER (*appeler*) ETER (*jeter*) YER (*nettoyer*) AYER (*payer*). And a few ER verbs will have an accent mark change.

I always remembered the accent *grave,* (grave accent) from the accent *aigu,* (acute accent) as the accent grave is the one pointing you forward, toward the grave. Ouch. Don't worry, you'll understand all about accent marks soon.

Let's add some useful IER verbs to our notebook, *que tu aimes,* When adding these verbs to your list, use our template. The *nous* is dropped off the chart as usual, and the *vous* will be moved to the bottom and the ER is dropped from all, always leaving the I.

Here's a sample IER verb in the present tense:

COPIER

Je copi**e**
Tu copi**es**
Il, elle, on copi**e**
Ils, elles copi**ent**
Vous copi**ez**

Here are a few more IER verbs that you'll want in your collection. First they're in their infinitive form, then using the template above you can break them down into the present tense. The following chart shows the pronunciation of the Kumbaya 7 and *vous* as they would sound in the present tense.

BTW, these are called infinitives they are in the infinitive or "infinite" state. They are everlasting. In this state they are not connected to a person, place, thing, time, nothing. They never change. (Oh, really? Never change? Yeh, until they change, which is all the time. Add a simple *je* and boom, they'll change like a… never mind. Hey, I don't make the rules.)

INFINITIVE	PRONOUNCED PRESENT TENSE, KUMBAYA 7,	VOUS
COPIER (To copy)	COPI	COPI-A
CRIER (To cry)	CRI	CRI-A
MODIFIER (To modify)	MODIFI	MODIFI-A
NÉGOCIER (To negotiate)	NÉGOCI	NÉGOCI-A
ÉTUDIER (To study)	ÉTUDI	ÉTUDI-A
OUBLIER (To forget)	OUBLI	OUBLI-A
VARIER (To vary)	VARI	VARI-A
SKIER (To ski)	SKI	SKI-A
SIMPLIFIER (To simplify)	SIMPLFI	SIMPLIFI-A
VÉRIFIER (To verify)	VÉRIFI	VÉRIFI-A

Remember, not a lone wolf anywhere. Forget about memorizing single words. Like, *étudier* is not simply to *study*. Remember *whole phrases*. As you grab your notebook, *que tu aimes*, you might say: *"J'aime étudier."* (I love to study.) We're simply using two of our known verbs here, one is the new IER verb, *étudier*, plus our previously learned ER verb *aimer*. Just for fun let's add a link word too. A simple *donc* will do. *Donc, j'aime étudier.* (So, I love to study).

Maybe you'll think: *J'aime varier ma vie.* (I like to vary my life.) That's two ER verbs: our new IER verb, *varier*, plus the present tense of *aimer*. And pick out a link word or two to add. Maybe even a suffix changer? See them?

Stick these IER verbs to your arsenal of ER candidates when out exploring Frenchville, perhaps at the supermarket or local coffee hang.

Now, hold on, I'm throwing in a long sentence in here. But wait till we break it down and you see what's in it. There's nothing that you haven't seen.

I'm in a Frenchville ski shop and here's what I'm thinking: ***De temps en temps, elle achète beaucoup de choses. Alors, je pense qu'elle aime skier.*** OMG ! That's a ton of writing. Too advanced! But no. (*Mais non!*) That might look like a ton of words, a big sentence, but break it down, there's absolutely NOTHING there that we didn't look at. It simply says: From time-to-time, she buys a lot of things. So, I think she likes to ski.

Look at the French sentence again. Break it down. This is super important. It's just 3 link words from your list, *de temps en temps, beaucoup, alors*. Personal pronouns are used 3 times: *elle, je, elle.* We've added 4 ER verbs that we've studied (one is an IER) and all are in the present tense: *acheter, penser, aimer*, and *skier*. Note: *Que elle* has become *qu'elle*, (that she) dropping the final E off *que* and replacing it with an apostrophe thus breaking up the weak vowels sounds so it's faster and smoother to say. (*Que* was in our list of nine mini consonant words that always contract around vowels. Look again: *Me, je, de, ce, le, ne, que, se.* Notice that *tu* is not on the list as it is often not contracted, as in the notebook, ***que tu aimes.***)

Voilà. These are two complete sentences. TWO SENTENCES and you have a good idea what they mean. Right? Even if you didn't at first, you'll get there. Write the French sentence with its translation in your notebook, *que tu aimes.*

You're on the inside of French now. A few simple link words from your list... a couple of regular ER verbs from the 1000's of regular ER verbs... plus one *je* and an *elle* used twice -- and we're speaking in sentences. You can compose endless sentences with what you've seen, plus the new vocabulary that you're collecting.

Don't worry if you got lost. If you're just reading through the book to get an idea of French, you may not have studied the link words and verb meanings. It's fine. Just get a footing here. See how we're breaking down each sentence into usable parts. Come back and study the words and links you need when ready. No pressure. Go at your own pace, at your own stage in learning.

Make sure you've got the correct pronunciation and say these sentences out loud. (Again Google translate is your friend for pronunciation).

Awaken the French actor in you and try to get the accent down, but don't stress. You're already dealing with *major* French!

Hold on. I hear something. Loud. I'd know that revving sound anywhere.

Vroom. Vroom. Vroom.

Well, well. Look who just raced up on his tricked out Harley. The one and only: *ALLER*. As usual he's a mess. Grease everywhere. His t-shirt's ripped, got worn leather chaps. He's not wearing a helmet -- yeah, it's the law here, but – hey, it's *ALLER*. He follows no rules, no laws. He's the lone outcast from the ER group, and he's not about to follow anybody. Yes this is that one rebel out of 999 conservative, law-abiding ER verbs, and he HATES rules.

ALLER is the original buck-the-system, do-your-own-thing bad boy. But he's one of those impressive guys you'll rely on *all day, every day* when speaking French.

Aller is your *go-to* guy when you want *to-go-to* anywhere. And nope, sorry, the Kumbaya clan can't help you with *aller* in the present tense, he's a *very irregular dude.*

ALLER (To go)	PRO- NOUNCED	TRANSLATION
Je vais	VAY	I go
Tu vas	VAH	You go
Il, elle, on va	VAH	He, she, it, one goes, or we go
Ils, elles vont	VON	They go
Vous allez	AL-A	You go (formal or you plural)

Use your powers of imagination and take *aller* out for a spin. *Aller* means *to go*. He loves *to go* out! *To go* anywhere! Add him to your list of other verbs, your growing vocabulary, and a few link words as you go about your day. Play with your French learning. Remember, always get the right pronunciation as you advance. Check with Google translate first, (put the icon on your home page for quick access) or Forvo or Rhinospike. Make sure you've got the correct, authentic sound before you set out to use it.

Frenchville starts at home. As you go about the house, narrate your own actions using *aller*. Out loud is always better, unless you're scaring people by talking to your front door in French. You might simply say: *Je vais à la salle de bain.* (I'm going to the bathroom.) *Je vais à la cuisine.* (I'm going to the kitchen). *Je vais chercher ma petite clé.* (I'm going to look for my little key). Remember, you've labeled items all over your house, right? Use them all.

Don't forget to crank it up a notch and add a few link words: *De temps en temps je vais à la salle de bain. (At time s (or from time to time) I go to the bathroom.) Ensuite, je vais à la cuisine. (*Then, I'm going to the kitchen.)

Finalement, je vais chercher ma petite clé. (Finally, I'm going to look for my little key.)

Now, off to the supermarket with *aller*. *Je vais au marché.* (I'm going to the market). *Généralement je vais regarder les gens.* (Generally I go watch people). Describe what you see, use your notebook, *que tu aimes,* if you need vocabulary. *L'homme va acheter une banane maintenant.* (The man is going to buy a banana now). *Premièrement, je vais manger une pomme.* (First, I'm going to eat an apple.) *Ils vont chercher sa voiture.* (They're going to look for their car.) Be *français* in your thoughts. Build a vivid Frenchville. Take it with you everywhere. Talk to, and about, the people, places and things all around you. Heck, sprinkle French into your daily conversations with friends and family. *C'est chic*!

Getting to know a bad boy more intimately.

We can't walk away from *ALLER* so quickly, he's much more than a pretty face; way more than a tough, tan, muscular, macho, rebel kinda guy. The dude doesn't disappoint. He's actually got superhero powers.... and *he's all about cheating. Aller* will help you cheat your way into the future tense.

By using *aller* in the present tense (*je vais, tu vas, il, elle, on va, ils, elles vont, vous allez*) and adding any verb -- *any verb* – ER, IR, RE – you're really talking about what *you're going to be doing.* This is a type of future tense. It's called the near future. It's not actually IN the future (I will be on Mars tomorrow) but it's getting you into the future (I will *be going* to Mars tomorrow).

Take *PARLER:* to use this ER verb in the true future tense you'd have to know the future tense word, *parlerai.* ***Je parlerai avec Cher dans trois jours.*** (I *will speak* to Cher in three days.) This is where ***aller***, our superhero, comes to the rescue. He can whisk you into the future before you've learned ONE future tense verb. That's pretty handy. (There's our word *pretty* again.)

Here's how you'd speak about the future using *aller's* superpowers:

Je vais *parler avec Philipe.* (I'm ***going to*** speak with Phillip.)

Vous allez *manger, finalement.* (You're ***going to*** eat, eventually.)

Tu vas *chercher Luis, lundi?* (Are you ***going to*** look for Luis on Monday?)

Ils vont *chez Florence dans trois jours.* (They're ***going to*** Florence's place in three days.)

Elle va *manger ça plus tard.* (She's gonna eat that later.)

This is all future activity – without knowing one verb in future tense. Take *aller* in the present tense, add any verb -- the whole, unchanged infinitive of any verb -- and *voilà!* You're in the future. It's the *aller* allure.

But hold on, it's easy to get lazy and buddy up with *aller* relying on him to always take you into the future. And he will, and he can, he's that kinda guy.

Je vais can easily become your favorite phrase. *Je vais faire ça.* (I'm gonna do this.) *Je vais faire cela .*(I'm gonna do that.) *Je vais. Je vais. Je vais.* Mix it up. Give the real-deal future words a chance sometimes, too. (Future tenses are my favorites as they're SO easy and they advance your communication from basic to much more advanced in no time. We'll be getting to them soon.)

***Au revoir* ER verbs. Time to move on. Nice meeting you. Boo-hoo. Sob. Sniffle, sniffle. Adieu.**

Sorry, I'm having a hard time moving on from present tense ER verbs. They're so easy to learn, and there are over 1000. So they're 1000% useful, and just… well… friendly verbs. Plus they come with their own kicked out superhero, *aller.*

But it's time to move on and struggle to learn all the top present tense verbs with IR and RE endings. Yikes. Then we can begrudgingly move on to even more obstinate verbs, like the many irregulars, future tenses, and the 4 or 5 chaotic past tenses. (My grammar loathing cerebral cortex is now in full glaze mode. But I'm kidding, it's not that bad. Don't get nervous.)

Yep, *au revoir* my dear ER verbs. Goodbye. So long. *Arrivederci! Ciao.* I bid you farewell.

But wait! Farewell? WHY? Because that's what lots of conjugation books do? Pssft! Could everyone be wrong about *that* order too. (Here I go again.) Is jumping from all top present tense verbs in ER, IR and RE, then on to all the past tenses, then all future tenses – then wherever – the way to go? Why can't we hang out here longer? Get to know the ER family even more. We're talking picnics, bar-b-ques, going to the state fair *ensemble*. We can take the ERs everywhere. Dagnabbit, YES! Let's stay. We're family now. Kumbaya family.

What's past is past – or is it?

When it comes to grammar -- I hate it all -- and past tenses are definitely top-notch, busting-at-the-seams, full-on *grammar*. Of course, there isn't just *one* past tense to keep life simple -- nope, they've piled on a few. (You'll be fine.)

Here's a sample:

Imparfait (Imperfect)

Passé composé (Compound past)

Passé simple (Simple past)

Plus-que-parfait (Pluperfect)

Passé Antérieur (Anterior past)

Plus there are a few more, just for fun. Confused? I am. I really like the *plus-que-parfait* past. (The *more than perfect* past?) Doesn't sound like anyone's past that I know. Then there's the *passé antérieur*. (Aren't all pasts -- *anterior*?) Best of all is the *l'imparfait*. (The *imperfect* past?) That's the only truthful one there; I'm sure we can all relate to an imperfect past. So that's who we're sticking with as among the easiest, *most honest*, and a very practical tense to learn.

SECRET: What if past tense ER verbs were *easier* to use than it's been alluded to? What if ALL the ER verbs – not just present tense – had the famous *letter dumps* we saw?

Remember how we tossed out the E, ES, and ENT sounds from the end of the spoken words? Here comes round two. Past tense, *l'imparfait* (imperfect) ER verbs are just as simple, using that same conjugation chart.

Nous has been kicked out, *vous* has fallen to the bottom of the chart -- and the rest of our happy Kumbaya family -- all pronounced with one sound – all back together again. Kumbaya!

L'imparfait is the was/were/used to verb tense. I was eating, he was talking, I was thinking. They were looking, they were parking, they were swimming. I used to ski, he used to race cars, they used to live in Hawaii. You can cover a lot of past territory using this easy tense. And it's got the perfect name. IMPARFAIT means IMPERFECT. It's earned that name too as it covers action that's kinda incomplete. It comes from the Latin word: *imperfectus*, meaning "unfinished." It's an ongoing, incomplete action or an action done over and over. So it's not really completed, or "perfect," it's "imperfect." Example "I killed a verb!" It's perfect, it's done, complete. (I knew one day I'd do it.) Compare that completed action to the *imparfait*: "I *was* killing a verb when it jumped up and ran way." (Darn!)

Donc, if you thought the present tense ER was easy to conjugate, (you *did* right?) wait till you see the trick in *l'imparfait tense*. *C'est vachement* brilliant! Hold on, this is going to blow your mind. Wait for it...

L'IMPARFAIT, ER VERBS:

PARLER (To speak/to talk)	PRONOUNCED	TRANSLATION
Je parl**ais**	PARL-A	I was speaking, used to speak
Tu parl**ais**	PARL-A	You were speaking, used to speak
Il, elle, on parl**ait**	PARL-A	He, she, it, one, we were speaking, used to speak
Ils,elles parl**aient**	PARL-A	They were speaking, used to speak
Vous parl**iez**	PARL-IA	You were speaking (formal, or you plural)

MANGER (To eat)	PRONOUNCED	TRANSLATION
Je mange**ais**	MANJ-A	I was eating, used to eat
Tu mange**ais**	MANJ-A	You were eating, used to eat
Il,elle,on mange**ait**	MANJ-A	He, she, it, one, we were eating, used to eat
Ils,elles mange**aient**	MANJ-A	They were eating, used to eat
Vous mang**iez**	MANG-IA	You were eating, used to (formal, or you plural)

Okay, I know – *manger* has a hiccup. It's an irregularly spelled *imparfait* verb. It's rare, but it does happen. Normally we drop the whole ER ending but in *manger,* we leave the E and then add on the final letters AIS. MANGEAIS. Ahh, but it's still pronounced like all the other ER verbs. The

Kumbaya family at work. In speaking, leaving the E there makes no difference. And after all, we're learning to speak, right?

AIMER (To love/to like)	PRONOUNCED	TRANSLATION
J'aim**ais**	AIM-A	I used to love, or like
Tu aim**ais**	AIM-A	You used to love, or like
Il,elle,on aim**ait**	AIM-A	He, she, it, one, we used to love, or like
Ils,elles aim**aient**	AIM-A	They used to love, or like
Vous aim**iez**	AIM-IA	You used to love, or like, (formal or you plural)

Notice anything super interesting about the three verbs above? All three verbs, *PARLER*, *MANGER*, and *AIMER*, with all their matching Kumbaya endings are ALL pronounced exactly like the word *IMPARFAIT* itself.

Wait—so *l'imparfait* verbs are pronounced exactly like the word *imparfait* itself! OMG! Brilliant! Are you kidding??? The name of the verb tense actually tells you what to do! Am I really the only one who figured this out? YES! And you guys chose to come along with me in this book! You're brilliant too! ☺ You rock. Look at the 7 member Kumbaya family below. I added the word *imparfait* to the sample chart just to see. It's part of the gang.

IMPARFAIT	*PRONOUNCED*
Imparfait	**MPARF-A**
Je parl**ais**	PARL-A
Tu aim**ais**	AIM-A
Il,elle,on habit**ait**	ABIT-A
Ils,elles dans**aient**	DANS-A

WHAT? Gotta repeat this as it's almost unbelievable…The ending of *all* ER verbs in our seven member Kumbaya family in *l'imparfait* – are pronounced exactly like the name of their tense's own name. Yes, *l'imparfait* = *l'MPARF-A*. (*Imparfait* is kinda pronounced MPARF-A).

Once again, the answer is right there. Job done for you! *Donc*, how do you pronounce the whole Kumbaya family in ER verbs in *l'imparfait*? Just like you pronounce the word *imparfait*! *Mparf-A*.

And more, that's not only in ER endings, you'll see it in IR and RE verbs too. Plus many *imparfait* conjugations will contain the same ending, *ait*, or similar endings of the word *imparfait* itself, a pattern you'll see, making it easy to recognize most *imparfait* verbs anywhere. (*Ai, ait, ais, aient*) These repeating letter combinations will tip you off: *Je jouais, il jouait, je finissais, tu finissais, elle finissait, tu vendais, ils vendaient, il vendait,* etc.). *L'imparfait* is like a convention hall of AI, AIS, AIT, and AIENT. (And of course let's not leave out our good friend *vous* and his IEZ ending.) Watch for these endings. You can easily recognize *l'imparfait* anywhere. Even the word *imparfait,* has the AIT.

DEMANDER (To ask)	PRONOUNCED
Je demand**ais**	DEMAND-A
Tu demand**ais**	DEMAND-A
Il, elle, on demand**ait**	DEMAND-A
Ils, elles demand**aient**	DEMAND-A
Vous demand**iez**	DEMAND-IA

DONNER (To give)	
Je donn**ais**	DONN-A
Tu donn**ais**	DONN-A
Il, elle, on donn**ait**	DONN-A
Ils, elles donn**aient**	DONN-A
Vous donn**iez**	DONN-IA

TRAVAILLER (To work)	
Je travail**lais**	TRAVAILL-A
Tu travail**lais**	TRAVAILL-A
Il, elle, on travail**lait**	TRAVAILL-A
Ils, elles travail**laient**	TRAVAILL-A
Vous travail**liez**	TRAVAILL-IA

PENSER (To think)	**PRONOUNCED**
Je pens**ais**	PENS-A
Tu pens**ais**	PENS-A
Il, elle, on pens**ait**	PENS-A
Ils, elles pens**aient**	PENS-A
Vous pens**iez**	PENS-IA

RESTER (to stay)	
Je rest**ais**	REST-A
Tu rest**ais**	REST-A
Il, elle, on rest**ait**	REST-A
Ils, elles rest**aient**	REST-A

TROUVER (To find)	
Je trouv**ais**	TROUV-A
Tu trouv**ais**	TROUV-A
Il, elle, on trouv**ait**	TROUV-A
Ils, elles trouv**aient**	TROUV-A
Vous trouv**iez**	TROUV-IA

HABITER (To live)	
J'habit**ais**	ABIT-A
Tu habit**ais**	ABIT-A
Il, elle, on habit**ait**	ABIT-A
Ils, elles habit**aient**	ABIT-A
Vous habit**iez**	ABIT-IA

MORE ER VERBS	IMPARFAIT - KUMBAYA 7,
CHANGER (To change)	CHANG-A
ÉCOUTER (To listen)	ÉCOUT-A
VISITER (To visit)	VISIT-A
CHERCHER (To look for)	CHERCH-A
JOUER (To play)	JOU-A
SIGNER (To sign)	SIGN-A
PASSER (To pass)	PASS-A
FABRIQUER (To make)	FABRIQ-A
PRÉFÉRER (To prefer)	PRÉFÉR-A
SEMBLER (To seem)	SEMBL-A
VOLER (To fly)	VOL-A
NAGER (To swim)	NAG-A
GOUTER (To taste)	GOUT-A
FERMER (To close)	FERM-A
ACHETER (To buy)	ACHET-A
LAVER (To wash)	LAV-A
SE LAVER (To wash yourself)	SE LAV-A

And where's our Bad Boy *aller*? How does he act in *l'imparfait*? Surprise, surprise, *aller* calms down in *l'imparfait* and acts just like all the rest of the ER verbs, using his root word. While in the present tense he's a wild and crazy guy, here he's back to his ER roots.

ALLER(To go)	**PRONOUNCED**	**TRANSLATION**
J'all**ais**	AL-A	I was going, used to go
Tu all**ais**	AL-A	You were going, used to go
Il,elle,on all**ait**	AL-A	He, she, it, one was, or we
Ils,elles all**aient**	AL-A	They were going
Vous alliez	AL-IA	We were going, you formal or you plural

66

Spelling tip: Notice with all the ER *imparfait* tenses above, the word *imparfait* itself has an *ai* in it. All of our Kumbaya ER family that we're keeping together (not *vous*, he's at the bottom) will always be spelled with an **AI** in them in *l'imparfait*, just like the word *imparfait* itself always has an AI in it.

If you remember our saying: **It's EZ and ESSENTIAL to ENTERTAIN ME...** the **EZ** and the **ENT** are still here in *l'imparfait*. *Vous* still has that **EZ** ending as it did in the present tense (*vous parlez, is now vous parliez*). And *Ils* and *elles* have both the new **AI** as found in the word *imparfait*—plus their usual **ENT** ending as they had in the present tense. (*Ils parlent*, is now *ils parlaient*). Again, this will never help if you're speaking but it could be useful if you have to write using the imperfect, or if you're reading.

When writing in *l'imparfait*, note that the *je* and *tu* verbs both end in **S**. Well of course old faithful **tu/stu** does. (*Je parlais, tu aimais*.)

Il, elle, and on end in a **T**. (*Il parlait, elle visitait, on aimait*). It's easy to get the spelling confused as endings are often not pronounced. With over 1000 ER verbs, this little tip might save you on a test someday. Remember: **S** comes before **T** in the alphabet, and on the ER *imparfait* charts. See below how the ending S comes before the endings in T.

Je parlai**S**

Tu parlai**S**

Il, elle, on parlai**T**

Yes, *je* and *tu* conjugated verbs often end in **S** – but will *NEVER* end in **T.**

Yes, *il, elle,* and *on* conjugated verbs often end in **T** -- but will *NEVER* end in **S.**

Never, not in any verb, not in any ending, not in any conjugation, never, anywhere.

Take another look at the *je parlais, tu parlais,* and the *il, elle, on parlait* above. Burn this into your memory. **S** comes before **T** in the alphabet, just like it does in the above conjugation of je, tu = **S** and il, elle = **T**.

Another spelling observation: Keep *an eye out*, you'll see that verbs conjugated for the personal pronoun *je* will often have and **ai** appearing somewhere in various tenses, not just in *l'imparfait. (Je vais, je parlais, j'irai, j'ai, etc.)* Okay, got it? So *je* often has an E, S or an AI hanging around its endings. (All good to know for French tests.)

Except for *vous* – we've seen there is only ONE sound used for each verb with the present tense ER verbs. The Kumbaya family. (EX: PARL, MANG, AIM). Same with *l'imparfait*, only ONE sound used for each verb, (EX: PARL-A, MANJ-A, AIM-A).

With the Kumbaya seven, *je, tu, il, elle, on, ils, elles* all having ONE SOUND FOR EACH VERB, in the present, or in *l'imparfait* -- you can grab any of the 1,000 ER verbs, even ones you've never heard of – and they'll all be pronounced the same, *exactly* like their stem for the present. (Parle = PARL) Or with the –A sound, for *l'imparfait*. (Parlais = PARL-A).

Back to the future.

With *aller* we've dipped our toes into the near future with his ability to convert most verbs into the *"going to"* mode. *(Je vais parler, tu vas manger, il va aimer.)*

Now let's jump full-fledged into the future tense – without *aller*'s superpowers. This is another French gift for you.

Take your favorite ER verb, use the complete infinitive, *the whole shebang*, yes, even keep the ER ending, then add these new endings, and BOOM you've landed 100% in the future. Again, these are my favorite tenses. It can be fun to take any *WHOLE* ER verb, and easily pop it right into the future with just a tiny change.

PARLER (To speak/to talk)	PRONOUNCED
Je parler**ai**	AI
Tu parler**as**	AH
Il, elle, on parler**a**	AH
Ils, elles parler**ont**	ON
Vous parler**ez**	A

Spelling Tip: Note the **S** ending with the *tu* again? *Tu parleras.* Yep it's our famous buddy Stu again. 99% of the time, *every* verb conjugated in *every* tense, *everywhere* for the personal pronoun *tu* will end in an **S**. Note the **AI** once again showing up with the *Je*?

In the future tense, *vous* has the same **EZ** ending that it had in the present tense, (*Parlez*), and in *l'imparfait,* (*Parliez*), so it's **EZ** to remember the spelling.

In the present tense the *ils* and *elles* ended in **ENT**, (*Parlent*). In *l'imparfait* they ended in **ENT** (*Parlaient*). But here in the future tense, **ONT**, (*Parleront*). It's the only place they change out their **ENT** ending.

MANGER (To eat)	PRONOUNCED
Je manger**ai**	MANJER-AI
Tu manger**as**	MANJER-AH
Il,elle,on manger**a**	MANJER-AH
Ils, elles manger**ont**	MANJER-ON
Vous manger**ez**	MANJER-A

AIMER (To love/to like)	PRONOUNCED
J'aimer**ai**	AIMER-AI
Tu aimer**as**	AIMER-AH
Il, elle, on aimer**a**	AIMER-AH
Ils, elles aimer**ont**	AIMER-ON
Vous aimer**ez**	AIMER-A

DEMANDER (To ask)	PRONOUNCED
Je demander**ai**	DEMANDER-AI
Tu demander**as**	DEMANDER-AH
Il, elle, on demander**a**	DEMANDER-AH
Ils, elles demander**ont**	DEMANDER-ON
Vous demander**ez**	DEMANDER-A

DONNER (To give)	PRONOUNCED
Je donner**ai**	DONNER-AI
Tu donner**as**	DONNER-AH
Il, elle, on donner**a**	DONNER-AH
Ils, elles donner**ont**	DONNER-ON
Vous donner**ez**	DONNER-A

From here you can add the pronunciations to the rest of these verbs. Just like above:

TRAVAILLER (To work)
Je travailler**ai**
Tu travailler**as**
Il, elle, on travailler**a**
Ils, elles travailler**ont**
Vous travailler**ez**

PENSER (To think)
Je penser**ai**
Tu penser**as**
Il, elle, on penser**a**
Ils, elles penser**ont**
Vous penser**ez**

RESTER (To rest)
Je rester**ai**
Tu rester**as**
Il, elle, on rester**a**
Ils, elles rester**ont**
Vous rester**ez**

TROUVER (To find)
Je trouver**ai**
Tu trouver**as**
Il, elle, on trouver**a**
Ils, elles trouver**ont**
Vous trouver**ez**

HABITER (To live)
J'habiter**ai**
Tu habiter**as**
Il, elle, on habiter**a**
Ils, elles habiter**ont**
Vous habiter**ez**
(Remember bye-bye H sound)

Below are the rest of the ER verbs that we've seen before in the present and *l'imparfait* tense. List these in your notebook too, *que tu aimes*, and fill out the future tense for each personal pronoun in each verb. (It's not homework, it's a suggestion that you should follow. Okay, it's homework.) Again, use the entire verb, and simply add the future endings. *Et voilà!*

CHANGER (To change)
ÉCOUTER (To listen)
VISITER (To visit)
CHERCHER (To look for)
JOUER (To play)
SIGNER (To sign)
PASSER (To pass)
FABRIQUER (To make)
PRÉFÉRER (To prefer)
SEMBLER (To seem)
VOLER (To fly)
NAGER (To swim)
GOUTER (To taste)
FERMER (To close)
ACHETER (To buy)
LAVER (To wash)

SE LAVER (To wash yourself)

And where's our bad boy *aller*? How does he behave in the future tense? Surprise, surprise, *aller* kicks into high gear, once again showing off his rebel streak, after taking a break and trying to fit in during *l'imparfait* tense, here he's gone nuts. (Or as we learned: *Il deviant chèvre* (He's become a goat). Hopefully you remember that saying, and it was written in your notebook, *que tu aimes.*

ALLER (To go)
J'ir**ai**
Tu ir**as**
Il, elle, on ir**a**
Ils, elles ir**ont**
Vous ir**ez**

Yep, I guess aller has really lost it with this IR bit above in the future tense. (IR also means *to go* in Spanish.)

Let's regroup a minute and take another look at the many faces of our buddy *ALLER*:

PRESENT
Je vais
Tu vas
Il, elle, on va
Ils, elles vont
Vous allez

L'IMPARFAIT
J'allais
Tu allais
Il, elle, on allait
Ils, elles allaient
Vous alliez

FUTURE
J'irai
Tu iras
Il, elle, on ira
Ils, elles iront
Vous irez

How are you doing so far? Are you confused, *perdu*? Are you okay*? Est-ce que ça va?* You've seen a ton of French in very few pages. I think it's time to...

STOP!
ARRÊTEZ.
LET'S SLOW DOWN.

Hopefully your notebook, *que tu aimes*, is filling up with tips, tricks, word sets, and verbs. Don't get frustrated. Take your time. Reread pages, go back, leaf through your notebook. Has your vocabulary list grown? Is your fridge labeled? Are you conversing in word sets with your front door? Have you visited Frenchville in your mind, applying *français* to the people, places, and things around you? *Petit à petit*, have you sprinkled a few of your favorite sticky rice links and expressions into your day?

Time to stop. *Arrêtez*. Slow down. Time to absorb everything. You've already learned a ton of ER verbs in various tenses. Let it sink in. Go back. Read through it all. Practice making sentences and say them out loud. Do you even realize how much territory you've covered already? A ton, so take a big break. Celebrate. You've done the hardest part, jumped right into the middle of French, full speed.

Let's recap. Here's what you've done:

You've received the first *new* verb chart that's been created in the last 384 years.

You've studied 36 top priority ER verbs that you'll need daily. (37 with our bad boy *aller*). You've met these verbs in the *present, l'imparfait and future tense*. Oh, and the *near future tense*, using *aller*'s superpower *going to*. Since the 'near' future is a real tense (go figure) -- that's 4 tenses so far. 4 tenses and 37 verbs. Look how far we've gotten and it wasn't that painful. You even understood full sentences about a lady buying ski clothes. (Understood? If not take another look.)

Let's calculate. 4 tenses X 37 verbs = 148 verbs. But with 7 times less work thanks to the Kumbaya family... that's 148 divided by 7, right? Or multiplied by 7? Added? I don't know, but that's a ton of verbs.

Hopefully you've found a few useful spelling tips. It's **ez** and **es**sential to **ent**ertain me. And *tu* we've nicknamed Stu.

You've learned about the poor lone wolf, lone word, and their precarious situation. You're using full blown expressions and phrases, because *no one* ever had a memorable conversation with a dictionary. (I was lonely and it was 86 proof tequila.)

Yes, by now (hopefully) you've got a notebook, *que tu aimes,* and you're filling it up with new word sets, links, expressions and you're taking these words out on jaunts to the supermarket, your job, out driving. Frenchville is alive and well. *Vive Frenchville.*

You may be carrying around a *verre bleu vide* or a match box car, or a red gummy bear and putting them through daily scenarios.

You've been introduced to the bad boy *aller*. He's an invaluable aide to help you speak French all day, every day. His superhero power is his ability to whisk you into the future with his "going to" mode. *Je vais... tu vas... il, elle, on va... ils, elles vont... vous allez au future avec aller! (Yes,* we're *all going to* the future with ***aller.***)

We've heard about the silent H and the nine mini consonants. (Look back if you're not sure what the minis are.)

You've faced the end – the suffixes matching so closely to English.

It's time to slow down; absorb it all before we move on to chapter two.

And if you're thinking, there's so much to learn how will I ever apply this? Don't worry, you'll get more familiar with the language as we go, and it'll all come together. Plus, we'll use WORD SAFARI later to focus on different aspects to help you remember. (Fun, promise.)

You're looking at a new language, from every angle, in just a few pages. New info is coming at you from all directions. It took centuries to develop this language. Centuries to refine it. We're condensing it into a small book. Take your time. Work on parts you need the most. If you're traveling, focus on the simple verbs so you can communicate. Ignore the info about spelling, accent marks, etc. Take what you need to communicate now. The info will always be here. I'm spewing it out so you have it for reference, not so you can perfectly memorize everything as you read it.

So whenever you're ready, take your time, and carry on. Hopefully you'll feel 100% settled with the first chapter before you move on. Don't rush it.

This time we're really saying goodbye to the ER verbs and bad boy *aller*. *Goodbye ER verbs. Ciao. Arrivederci. Au revoir. Adios.* Parting is such sweet sorrow. (Never mind.)

PART TWO

A Love Story,
an Arch Enemy,
and a Train Ride.

TWO

Confession time. I'm in love with a verb. Me. The world's foremost grammar hater, in love with a verb. And he's a *real* bad boy. We're talking, the Billy the Kid of verbs. He's among the most powerful, most influential, most hardworking verbs that you'll ever meet. Along with his buddy ***aller,*** he's the verb that you'll hang out with most of the time. Yes, this is the verb that will get you through your toughest French conversations *always*. This is the verb that you cannot live without. Be still my heart.

AVOIR: A LOVE STORY.

AVOIR is from the other side of the tracks from the goody-goody ER verbs. Even though *avoir* ends in IR, he's so rebellious, he's even from the other side of the tracks from his *own* IR family of verbs. (Would that put him back on the ER side of the tracks?)

Avoir is the heartthrob of *every* verb. (Every verb except one, and that's another bad boy you'll soon meet.) The mighty *avoir* is the superhero who's needed by almost everyone and he'll join up with ER, IR, and RE verbs. He has no boundaries. Tough and relentless, he's at the top of the MOST WANTED LIST for all French verbs. His superpowers are *almost* unmatched. (Except by... well... there is that one arch enemy.) Before we get to his superpowers, let's see how he looks in the present tense. Remember he's irregular, but of course he is -- he's a one-of-a-kind guy, so we expect that.

AVOIR (To have)	PRONOUNCED
J'**ai**	AY
Tu **as**	AH
Il, elle, on **a**	AH
Ils, elles **ont**	ON
Vous av**ez**	AV-A

Hold a sec. For some these few pages can be a tad tougher. It's okay. Irregular verbs can be some of the most difficult things you'll learn in any language. And if this is among the *most* difficult, that's great news. You'll be fine. Soon we'll be back to much more fun, dealing with new quirky irregular verbs and their crazy schemes.)

Back to *avoir*. You'll quickly get accustomed to him as you'll be using his skills everywhere. He's the most helpful verb in French, and will even be used to conjugate other verbs. (That's his super superpower.)

Lots of common expressions used daily *en français,* include *avoir* in their structure. Talk of sticky rice. *Avoir* is more like super glue of the French language. How did we live without him?

Here's *avoir* at his idiomatic best. Let's start with *IL Y A*. You'll use this all day long. It literally translates as IT HAS THERE. So *forget* that literal meaning. (Please!) Don't look at *IL Y A* as if it's three words. No. Think of it as just one word -- spelled funny, yes -- but just one word. (Avoir is hiding there in the letter A.)

IL Y A is simply -- *there is* or *there are*. That's it. Simple. *There is* or *there are*. Endless usage. A needed vocabulary gem to throw into your sentences daily.

There are three dogs.	**Il y a** trois chiens
There is a bridge.	**Il y a** un pont
There are four things to do.	**Il y a** quatre choses à faire
There's a better way.	**Il y a** une meilleure façon
There are problems.	**Il y a** des problèmes

Il y a can also *représente* time passage, meaning "ago." Simply use *il y a then* follow it with any amount of time and it transforms into *ago*. When did you live in France? *Il y a trois mois.* (Three months AGO.) When did you leave? *Il y a cinq minutes.* (Five minutes AGO).

There's another way of looking back in time and that confuses people. It's *depuis*. But that means *since* or *for*. *Depuis* is time related, but very different from the word *ago*. How long have you been studying French? *Depuis 15 jours.* (For 15 days) Or *depuis lundi* (Since Monday). Since, or for, = *depuis*. Time ago = *il y a*.) But we use both *ago* and *since* in English and it's no different in usage, so no problem. You can easily get confused when to use *il y a* vs. *depuis*. When speaking of time, I remember *Il Y A* as *Il Y AGO*.

I think of the following **A** as AGO so I know that's right. So *Il y A trois ans* = 3 years AGO.

Like all languages, French uses lots of shortcuts. *IL Y A* is often shortened to *YA*. "*Ya cinq ans j'ai gagné à la loterie.*" (Five years ago I won the lottery.) French speakers have to learn shortcuts to English phrases too, like "I have to go," which becomes, "Gotta go!" There are countless shortcuts everywhere, in every language, but that's the beauty of language, it's ever changing along with us.

Besides being part of the omnipresent *il y a* trio -- *avoir* shows up in many French expressions. While in English we say WE ARE things (I AM hungry, I AM thirsty, I AM 15 years old, I AM cold). In French they HAVE things (I HAVE hunger *(J'ai faim)*, I HAVE thirst, *(J'ai soif)*, I HAVE 15 years *(J'ai 15 ans)*, I HAVE coldness. *(J'ai froid)*. That's our *avoir* superhero at work.

The French see our use of I AM as very odd. I AM REMY, yes, that's me, that's who I am. But I AM HUNGRY? *That's who I am?* If you think about it -- it's more logical to say *I HAVE* hunger, than to say I AM hunger. It's as if you morphed into something else. That's why you shouldn't think in English and speak in French. You must think in French, to speak in French, or you'll be caught in a whirlwind of confusion.

As *avoir* is one of the most common, most flexible verbs, this superhero turns up in lots of expressions. For example, to be hot or cold *always* uses *avoir. J'ai froid, tu as chaud.* Here are more idioms that *must* use *avoir.*
Don't stress here, like with our chart full of link words, pick a few you'll use now, and save the rest.

Avoir besoin de	To need	**J'ai** envie de crêpes ce soir
Avoir chaud	To be hot	**Tu as** chaud?
Avoir froid	To be cold	Moi, **j'ai** froid.
Avoir sommeil	To be tired	**Il a** sommeil maintenant.
Avoir confiance en	To trust	**Elles ont** confiance en vous
Avoir de la chance	To be lucky	**Tu as** toujours de la chance
Avoir envie de	To want to	**J'ai** envie d'aller au cinéma
Avoir faim	To be hungry	**Il a** faim depuis 2 heures. (Remember depuis?)
Avoir soif	To be thirsty	**Ils ont** soif.
Avoir l'habitude de	To tend to	**J'ai** l'habitude de manger trop.
Avoir raison	To be right	**Vous avez** raison.
Avoir peur	To be afraid	**On a** peur de voler.
Avoir mal au	To be sick	**J'ai** mal à la tête.
Avoir horreur de	To detest	**J'ai** horreur des devoirs.
Avoir l'air	To seem	**Vous avez** l'air un peu snob.

For me *avoir l'air* from the list above, (to have *the air)* is French at its finest. It's a visual way to describe someone, or something. It's the way something seems or looks. *Elle a l'air mystérieuse* (She *seems* mysterious.) *Tu as l'air heureuse* (You seem happy.) *Le gâteau a l'air délicieux.* (The cake *looks* delicious). There is also the word that we learned with our ER verbs, *sembler* (to seem) but come on – *l'air* has *sembler* beat any day.

We have similar expressions when we say, "He has a certain air about him," or "She's putting on airs." But unlike our *very* occasional use, *l'air* is used constantly in French. CONSTANTLY. It just means SEEMS! And you know how often you use SEEMS in English. Same thing in French. It's a go to expression. Or so it *seems* to be. Learn it and you can describe anything.

If I were a teacher, right now I'd give you *devoirs* (homework) and ask you to write out sentences using the some *avoir* expressions above, plus add those sticky rice link words you've hopefully saved in your notebook, *que tu aimes*. Here are some *avoir* uses: *Généralement, **j'ai** raison.* (I'm usually right) Or... *De temps en temps **j'ai** peur de mon chat.* (Sometimes I'm afraid of my cat.) Or... *Bien sûr, **tu as l'air** extravagant ce soir.* (Of course, you look extravagant tonight.) But I'm not your French teacher and ***j'ai** horreur des devoirs* (I hate homework) so you're safe. Though, it would be very beneficial to try that. Just saying...

How is bad boy *avoir* used in a past tense? First, let's look at *l'imparfait*. This is the HAD, WAS HAVING, USED TO HAVE verb tense. Just like with our ER verbs, the Kumbaya family is alive and well – and as usual -- all pronounced the same.

IMPARFAIT	PRONOUNCED
J'av**ais**	AV-A
Tu av**ais**	AV-A
Il, elle, on av**ait**	AV-A
Ils, elles av**aient**	AV-A
Vous av**iez**	AV-IA

Nothing too difficult there. With a little practice *avoir* is easy to remember. Make sure you apply *avoir* on your Frenchville excursions... or with your French speaking partner... or anywhere you listen to, and preferably speak, French.

But to understand *avoir's* true superpowers, we've got to go back and join him in the present tense again. (This is why I love *avoir*.) *Avoir in the present tense* – is your key to using almost every verb – *in the past tense*! Confused? Nah, it's simple. Start with *avoir* in the present tense…

PRESENT TENSE, AVOIR (To have)
J'**ai**
Tu **as**
Il, elle, on **a**
Ils, elles **ont**
Vous av**ez**

Using *avoir* as seen here, in the present tense, he can also become an auxiliary verb, a helping hand. This is our key to getting straight back into the past tense, the *passé composé*. (*Composé* just means composed; this tense is *composed* of various elements such as *avoir* plus another verb and together, hand-in-hand, they step into the past.) Funny, *aller* takes us to the future, and *avoir* takes us to the past. They're both superheroes.

PASSÉ COMPOSÉ	PRONOUNCED	TRANSLATION
J'**ai** parlé	PARL-A	I spoke
Tu **as** mangé	MANJ-A	You ate
Il **a** aimé	AIM-A	He loved, or liked
Elle **a** voyagé	VOYAG-A	She travelled
On **a** demandé	DEMAND-A	We asked
Ils **ont** cherché	CHERCH-A	They looked
Elles **ont** travaillé	TRAVAILL-A	They worked
Vous **avez** donné	DONN-A	You gave (formal, or you plural)

MIND BLOWN. You can use *avoir's* superpower and go back in time by setting him up with just about ANY verb. (*Just about* any verb. Except, well, still to come – his one arch enemy, one more bad boy…)

Here's a quiz:

I've put *parler* below in two past tenses, *l'imparfait* (WAS/WERE/USED TO... I *was* talking to Bob,) and the *passé composé* (HAD... I *had talked* to Bob) which uses *avoir* as a helping hand. (Remember, *composé* just mean composed. It's composed of assorted elements here.)

Notice anything special about these two lists?

PARLER, L'IMPARFAIT
Je parlais
Tu parlais
Il, elle, on parlait
Ils, elles parlaient
Vous parliez

PARLER, PASSÉ COMPOSÉ
J'ai parlé
Tu as parlé
Il, elle, on a parlé
Ils, elles ont parlé
Vous avez parlé

See anything unusual?

Hint: We've been here before at the beginning of this book when I had a quiz about *parler, manger,* and *aimer.* I listed them all in the present tense and asked you what special about them and why they would make learning French easy.

Do you get what's interesting above?

All of these conjugated verbs, whether in *je, tu, il, elle, on, elle, ils,* or *elles* -- the entire Kumbaya family -- whether in *l'imparfait* or the *passé composé* -- even though all are written differently – you got it -- ALL SOUND THE SAME.

That's crazy! *C'est vachement fou*! There was definitely a verb wizard at the French Academy. Yes, pronounced exactly the same.

WHAT? HOW IS THAT POSSIBLE? So again you can learn one sound and be speaking in two past tenses?

You could use *l'imparfait* to say "*Je **parlais** en class.*" (I was speaking in class.) Or the *passé composé* and say "*J'ai **parlé** en class.*" (I spoke in class). *Parlais,* and *parlé* – and even the infinitive *parler,* though all written differently – *sound the same.* (*Vous,* not part of the Kumbaya clan, is pronounced a bit differently in *l'imparfait* as you hear the "i" sound in *vous parliez.*)

You don't have to strain your brain and remember two completely different sounding charts full of verbs to speak in the past tense. As these conjugated verbs, from the Kumbaya family *all sound the same* – it's harder to make a mistake. Less to memorize.

This is crazy. *C'est fou!* Thank you, French Academy – you made it possible to pronounce hundreds of different verbs -- conjugated in many different ways -- with *completely different spellings* and have them ALL SOUND THE SAME! How did you do that?

We just saw *parler,* here's *manger* and *aimer* in *l'imparfait* and *passé composé.* Bring all your ER verbs over and plug them in, they'll all sound the same. Talk of letter drop – look at *ils, elles mangeaient* below. We're dropping 5 letter sounds and leaving a simple **A** sound. (NOTE: Pronunciation varies from region to region. Some will say they do not sound *exactly* the same, others will say they do. You're fine.)

MANGER, L'IMPARFAIT (WAS/WERE/USED TO)	PRONOUNCED
Je mange**ais**	MANJ-A
Tu mange**ais**	MANJ-A
Il, elle, on mange**ait**	MANJ-A
Ils, elles mange**aient**	MANJ-A
Vous mang**iez**	MANJ-IA

MANGER, PASSÉ COMPOSÉ (HAD)	PRONOUNCED
J'ai mang**é**	MANJ-A
Tu as mang**é**	MANJ-A
Il, elle, on a mang**é**	MANJ-A
Ils, elles ont mang**é**	MANJ-A
Vous avez mang**é**	MANJ-A

AIMER, L'IMPARFAIT (WAS/WERE/USED TO)	PRONOUNCED
J'aim**ais**	AIM-A
Tu aim**ais**	AIM-A
Il, elle, on aim**ait**	AIM-A
Ils, elles aim**aient**	AIM-A
Vous aim**iez**	AIM-IA

AIMER, PASSÉ COMPOSÉ (HAD)	PRONOUNCED
J'ai aim**é**	AIM-A
Tu as aim**é**	AIM-A
Il, elle, on a aim**é**	AIM-A
Ils, elles ont aim**é**	AIM-A
Vous avez aim**é**	AIM-A

Time to look at the future tense with *avoir*. (Will have). If you look back at any future tense here, or anywhere, EVER, the personal pronouns, the Kumbaya family, will all have the same endings. The ai, as, a, ont, and ez are omnipresent. If it's the future tense, these are always the endings for ER, IR, or RE verbs, doesn't matter what verb *"So we got that going for us... which is nice."* (Sorry, old movie quote).

Avoir himself, all alone, will also be used to speak in the future, not just as a helping hand for verbs in the *passé composé*.

FUTURE, AVOIR
J'aur**ai**
Tu aur**as**
Il, elle, on aur**a**
Ils, elles, on aur**ont**
Vous aur**ez**

Not much to say here. By now you should be able to figure out the pronunciation. As usual with most French words, you'll be dropping the consonant sound from the word endings. You won't hear the **S, T** or **Z** from the *auras, auront,* and *aurez.*

Here's a question. Why would the French language be created with *so many* consonant endings, just to drop them all when speaking? Seems like a waste of packaging. Hmm. Over centuries French evolved from its Latin origins. Unlike other romance languages, French speakers began dropping the final sounds. But they're there in spelling, and do appear when needed to help out the wallflowers. They'll form liaisons with weak vowels and make the language stronger, sound better, easier to pronounce.

Wait – so basically the strong, often silent consonants sit it out until needed, and only then step in? Could it be? Genius! Like our *nous* and *vous*, remember they have no final consonant sound ever. They're pronounced "new" and "vew." But throw in a wallflower, a weak, floundering word starting with a vowel after them – like *allons*, or *allez*, and boom, those consonants are on their feet faster than flamenco dancers on Adderall. *Vous* rushes in as ***VOUZ.***

And *nous* jumps in as **NOUZ!** *Vouzzzz avez. Nouzzzz allons.* If that's true, French Academy, you get major points for this. But you sure do keep secrets. I tried to find out the answer as to why so many letters are dropped in French and not other romance languages, and the best I could do was that over the last 1,000 years the French began to pronounce the final letters less and less and less. Yeah, no kidding.

Speaking of *vous,* as usual with every conjugation, *vous* has an **EZ** with him added to all verb stems. *Vous* is an interesting guy. Notice he always has an **EZ** with him? It's his security blanket, he doesn't leave home without it. I'd say that 100 % of the time he has that **EZ** with him. (In the obscure *passé simple* and *passé antérieur* he'll show up with an **S** instead of his beloved **EZ.** But these tenses are used for formal and historical works, so don't worry about them.) Always make sure *vous* has his **EZ** security blanket for every conjugation, every time, everywhere. (Of course there is one major exception. Yes, there's one important place you'll be using where he'll never be escorted by an **EZ**…. one holy place… you'll see.) And again, when I reference all these spelling issues, most only matter in the written form. You're fine speaking without thinking of any of this. What a relief!

And *comme d'habitude,* there's that friendly **S** hanging around *tu*… aka Stu.

Ils and *elles* are our "**ent**ertaining" ENT group. (It's **EZ** and **ES**SENTIAL to **ENT**ERTAIN ME.) Like *vous,* who's hung up on his **EZ** ending, *ils* and *elles* in **ER** verbs don't leave home without their entourage of ENT. (Have you noticed that even entourage starts with an ENT? Of course you did.) The ENT paparazzi follow the *il*s and *elles.* TRUST it that the ENT crew will be with them. (*Parlent, aimaient, ferment, pensaient, donnent.*)

Okay, hold on – there *are* a few places where they'll dump their **ENT** entourage and show up with an **ONT**. One place is in ALL future tenses for the *ils* and *elles:* **ils, elles *ont*, ils, elles *parleront, mangeront, donneront*.**

Darn, that was looking so good, so easy, all pure ENTs everywhere before. Then boom the ONT was slipped in. But 99% of the time you'll be correct spelling all their stems with an ENT ending. (I stress all these spellings as you will not hear these sounds when spoken, so it can be hard to remember what they look like. This will help you recognize them when reading and writing, or on TV subtitles, plus you might need to ace a test someday.)

When watching Netflix, it's great to see the endings on verbs. I recently watched a French film and wasn't sure what the actor said, but as the subtitles flashed by I saw the ONT ending on a verb and knew he was speaking about the future and *ils*, or *elles*.

Once again, the future tense for ALL verbs, even ALL bad boys, and ALL irregulars, whether ER, IER, RE or IR verbs, will ALWAYS end in AI, AS, A, ONT, EZ.

As far as the ONT for *ils* and *elles* in their future tense – when they've always used ENT -- it's simple enough to remember the new ONT ending. But of course, I love puzzles, so here's how I remember it. (Here I go again.) ONT is in the future. How do you write and pronounce future in French? *FUTOR*. (Hold on French spelling experts.) Futor has an O, ONT has an O, hey, it's a match to me. *Ils* and *elles* usually show up with ENT… but in the FUTOR only, there's an O… an ONT. (Remember my mother thought I was a genius and my father thought… well… he might win here.)

No wait, my mother wins here! You see "future" in French is really spelled *FUTUR*, but that doesn't help us, right? But *FUTUR* kinda sounds like *FUTOR* when you say it, and if you remember it as *FUTOR*, with that O, you will get every spelling -- of every future tense word -- in the *ils* and *elles* category -- correct -- forever. That's a small price to pay for learning to spell *futor* incorrectly.

So in the future, when conjugating in the future, think of the French word *FUTUR* as *FUTOR*. It's not exactly kosher, but spelling *FUTUR* wrong will cure the *ils* and *elles* of their ENT problem. The O in *FUTOR* will hopefully remind you to use the ONT in all their future conjugations. If nothing else, I made such a big deal out of this, you might remember it anyway. That's all I've got about *avoir* and verb endings in the future tense. Can't help you anymore, sometimes you've just gotta bite the bullet and memorize, memorize, memorize. (Bite the bullet? English, always vivid).

Until you've got the *avoir* future tense conquered, you can always rely on our bad boy *aller*. Remember his superpower? He brings us into the future with *going to. Je vais, tu vas, il, elle, on va, ils, elles vont, vous allez.* When you're stuck not knowing the correct future word like, *je parlerai,* borrow *aller's* superpower. (We're about to have two superpowers work together for the first time. *Avoir* and *aller. Tu **vas avoir** mal de tête.* (You're **going to have** a headache.)

Be careful, don't lean on *aller* all the time to whisk you into the future. It's easy to get lazy and skip learning the real-deal future tense. It happens.

Everything becomes *je vais. Je vais faire ça… je vais faire cela… je vais là… Je vais. Je vais. Je vais.* Mix it up. If you're thinking, *je vais chez moi,* (I'm going home) add, *oui, **j'irai** chez moi.* Or *je vais manger plus tard, (I'm going to eat later)* add, *oui, je **mangerai** plus tard.* Future tenses are super easy, give them a chance.

Nothing like having two bad boy superpowers help us learn French. Can't lose.

A final look at *avoir* in four tenses:

AVOIR (To have)

PRESENT	PRONOUNCED	TRANSLATION
J'**ai**	AI	I have
Tu **as**	AH	You have
Il, elle, on **a**	A	He, she, it, one has, or we have
Ils, elles **ont**	ON	They have
Vous **avez**	AV-A	You have (formal, or you plural)

IMPARFAIT	PRONOUNCED
J'av**ais**	AV-A
Tu av**ais**	AV-A
Il, elle, on av**ait**	AV-A
Ils, elles av**aient**	AV-A
Vous av**iez**	AV-IA

PASSÉ COMPOSÉ	PRONOUNCED
J'**ai** eu	EU
Tu **as** eu	EU
Il, elle, on **a** eu	EU
Ils, elles **ont** eu	EU
Vous **avez** eu	EU

FUTURE	PRO-NOUNCED	TRANSLATION
Jaur**ai**	AUR-AI	I will have
Tu aur**as**	AUR-A	You will have
Il, elle, on aur**a**	AUR-A	He, she, it, one, we will have
Ils, elles aur**ont**	AURON	They will have
Vous aur**ez**	AUR-A	You will have (formal, you plural)

Since *avoir* has an IR ending, it would be a great time to introduce the rest of his small but notable IR family. But as we know, *avoir*, like *aller*, is a black sheep, renegade, bad boy, and doesn't fit into any family. I bet he'd rather skip this IR family reunion for now. Yep, he's left the building.

Instead, it's a good time to invite someone else to this party. Another bad boy. A bad boy who is often at odds with *avoir*. You might say he's the nemesis of *avoir*. The arch enemy of *avoir*. (More gossip, cool!)

This bad boy is so powerful, such royalty, that even the powerful *avoir* will never be as famous. And while these two don't always get along -- they sometimes have to work together. But surprise, surprise, this bad boy -- is actually -- a *bad girl*! Yes! *Être* is a *she*. She's usually thrown in with the RE verbs, but we know better. Like *aller* and *avoir* – she's out on her own stirring up trouble.

Here she is, *ÊTRE*. And boy, does she have superpowers. But alas, *être* is a verb monarch, royalty, a queen, and as you'll see, she has taken away a lot of *avoir's* power.

Être is all about her, and you, and me, and them, and everybody, and who we ARE. (I am, you are, they are…) While *avoir* had things (to have), and *aller* was going places (to go), *être* is all about being (to be, like I am, or you are, or it is…). She's a bright, heady, fascinating, powerful verb. She even has her own tense, well not really a whole tense, a half a tense. (One of her superpowers was so important that I thought she deserved way more recognition than the Academy had given her.) And yes, with all of her talents – and her royal pedigree -- which you'll find out about, of course she'll never follow in the footsteps of others. She's a super rebel. Here she is, going rogue in the present tense.

ÊTRE (To be)	PRONOUNCED	TRANSLATION
Je **suis**	SWI	I am
Tu **es**	EH	You are
Il, elle, on **est**	EH	He, she, it, one is, or we are
Ils, elles **sont**	SON	They are
Vous **êtes**	ET	You are (formal or you plural)

Can you believe it? Where does she come up with a *suis, est,* and *sont* from the word *être*? And look at *vous*! Remember him with his **EZ** security blanket? Here he is with a simple **S**. What's that about? (I had told you earlier there was *only one* place where *vous* leaves his **EZ** behind and shows up with an **S**. This is it.) Only *être* could get him to change his ways. She even gave him a mini crown for dropping his EZ security blanket – look he's got a circumflex. See it above the **e**. Vous êtes. This has *really* annoyed the crownless *avoir,* the verb "to have" everything.

This present tense chart is super important not only because you'll need these verbs to be talking about yourself all day long, (don't be that person) but because it's also a big part of *être's* superpower. Ready?

Ta-dah – introducing one of her superpowers and it's my favorite word set ever, the three words you will be using all day long. The one, the only, the famous, the magical: *EN TRAIN DE*!

This is one train you definitely want to jump aboard. It's part of an expression that means 'in the process of,' and used when going to do something, anything, everything. It's the French version of our English ING ending. Playing, walking, sitting, asking, eating, moving, thinking, even writing. (Which I'm *doing* right now. Even the word *doing* has an *ing*. It's everywhere.)

Je suis **en train de** manger des crêpes.	I'm eating crêpes
Tu es **en train de** penser à mon livre.	You are thinking of my book (thanks!)
Il est **en train de** partir?	He's leaving
Elle est **en train d'**acheter une maison	She's buying a house
On est **en train de** sortir ensemble.	We're going out together
Ils sont **en train de** jouer	They're playing
Vous êtes **en train de** vous marier	You are getting married

Notice, almost every verb in English has an ING ending. Eating, thinking, leaving, buying, going, playing, getting...

En train de is not a verb tense. The French don't have a "present progressive tense" like we do in English. (An ING ending.) Missing that, they must use their regular present tense to cover it. *Je mange* means both I eat, and I'm eating. *Je parle,* I speak, and I'm speaking. *Je étudier*, I study, or I'm studying. (*Je etudier* becomes *J'étudier*, right?)

But wait – can't be. NAH! I don't buy it. Seems like one tense doesn't cover it. To me, I eat and I'm eating are two completely different things and should be spoken in two different ways, not both filed under *je mange*. Sorry French Academy while you did an amazing job giving us letter dumps, you lost points on this one.

Due to this lack -- I hereby anoint **EN TRAIN DE** with its very own verb classification. I officially decree, in the name of Napoléon, the Duke of Perrier, and the French Parliament, that *EN TRAIN DE* shall be bestowed with one half of a verb tense point. Yes, one half. Therefore, we will be learning 4.5 tenses. *Present. Imparfait. Passé Composé, Future* and -- *en train de.* Congratulations *EN TRAIN DE!* Clap, clap, clap. Confetti flies everywhere. You'll use *en train de* all day long! It's a life saver to communicate.

Let's see what *être* is up to in *l'imparfait.* If you remember our bad boys *aller* and *avoir* were wild in the present tense. They broke all the rules. They were rebell**ious**. (Rebell**eux,** remember the suffix ending for English words ending in **ous,** become**s eux?**) *Aller* became *je vais,* and *avoir* showed up as *j'ai.* Then they calmed down in *l'imparfait,* using their stems to create a recognizable verb tense. *Aller* was *je allais*, while *avoir* was *je avais.* Reasonable. (Of course apostrophes had to jump in to help :*J'allais, j'avais)*

Now, *être,* what will she do in *l'imparfait…?*

IMPARFAIT (WAS, WERE, USED TO)

ÊTRE (To be)	PRONOUNCED	TRANSLATION
J'ét**ais**	ET	I was, used to be
T'ét**ais**	ET	You were, used to be
Il, elle, on ét**ait**	ET	He, she, it, one was, we were, or, used to be
Ils, elles ét**aient**	ET	They were, used to be
Vous ét**iez**	ET-IA	You were, used to be (formal, or you plural)

Not bad. She's back to her roots. At least we can recognize *être* here. Seems like all the rebels calmed down in *l'imparfait.* Hey, bucking the system can be tiring. (Of course we rebels know that.)

Take some time to buddy up with *être.* You'll rely on her all day, every day. (BTW: Notice above the *T'étais*? The T consonant in *Tu étais* shoved the U out of the way and rushed in to help wallflower *étais* to make the pronunciation smoother. (The missing U was replaced by an apostrophe to show us that something was removed.) *T'étais* is faster and cleaner sounding than *tu étais.*

And yes, French people notice when you don't make a liaison. *Je étais, (j'étais) je aime, (j'aime) je ai, (j'ai)* sound as horrible to a Frenchie as an English speaker feels about hearing: a eagle, a apple, a egg.

Now let's get to some gossip. The lifelong feud between *avoir* and *être*. Why? What's that all about? Why would *avoir* care what *être* does? There are a few things going on. Ready?

First, I love *avoir*, I've admitted it. But he's a verb. And all verbs have issues. *Avoir* is the *to have* verb, so he loves *to have* things. And *être* has something he will never have: A crown. An accent circumflex. (Hey, they're verbs, accent marks are *very* prestigious to verbs.) The circumflex usually shows that the letter **S** was removed sometime over the last 500 years, and the little crown accent took its place. Forest became *fôret*. Hospital, *hôpital*. Coast, *côte*, etc.

Speaking of accents -- I know I was in the middle of some great *avoir, être* gossip, but first here's a quick rundown of *the rest* of the French accents. A simple accent mark can make the difference between a sinner (a pécheur) and a fisherman, (a pêcheur).

Of the remaining four accent marks, after the circumflex, all are used with vowels, except one, which goes with the consonant **C**. The *cédille*, **Ç** turns the **C** sound into an **S** sound. It even looks like an **S**. (*Français, garçon, leçon.*)

The accent *grave*, the one pointing right, towards the grave, can slightly change the sound of a vowel but it's mostly to distinguish different meanings between matching words, like: *La* vs. *là*, (*the* vs. *over there*). *Ou* vs. *où*. (*or* vs. *where*). *A* vs. *à*, (*has* vs. *to*).

The accent *aigu* only shows up over the letter **E**, and makes a slight difference in pronunciation. The *aigu* or acute accent is used about 80% more than the *grave*. So unless you're trying to differentiate between *la* and *là* – or very few other words, it'll usually be the accent *aigu* and only over an **E**. (I mix up the *aigu*, tossing the accent over the wrong letters at times, like dropping it on a random letter A. Here's what I do to know it ONLY goes over an E –

which I am SURE no one else has to do. I think of the AIGU as a -GOOEY! (Almost the same pronunciation as *Aigu*.) It sticks to Es. It's **a goo-EEY** accent, hear the E in goo-ee?) So I remember that *aigu* is a "goo-**EEY**" accent and sticks to E's. And remember accents are hard for native speakers of other languages. Honestly, I'm wrong half the time, or leave accents off, or have my accent facing the wrong way. It's a minefield, or better said, a mindfield. You'll never stop learning a new language's fine points. I'd worry about speaking, more than accent marks.

The *trëma* helps separate the sound of two vowels, which in French vowel sounds normally join together. *Noel* is pronounced NOWELL without an accent. But with the *trëma* it becomes *noël,* and is pronounced NO...EL.

The word *mais* (meaning but) is pronounced MAI without an accent, but with the *trëma* it becomes *maïs,*(corn) pronounced as two sounds, MY ESSS. MY...ESSS has a big pause sound in the middle. The two dots of the trëma gives it that pause.

By the way there is some debate as to whether capital letters should get accent marks. According to the French Academy they must have accent marks. Not only can it change the meaning of a word, but the accent mark is part of the spelling of a word, so without them, you are spelling the word incorrectly. The Academy has spoken! But they are often left off anyway.

Now, back to the gossip, the feud between *avoir* and *être.*

Être was granted a circumflex crown for being the number one most important and most useful verb in all of the French kingdom-- and *avoir* never got over it. As the verb *to have,* if there was one thing *avoir* wanted to have, it was to have her diamond and emerald encrusted circumflex crown.

But the feud was WAY bigger than that. While *être* had the crown, *avoir* had the superpower to join up with 1000's of French verbs and form the *passé composé.* 1000's of verbs. Pick a verb, almost any verb, and good chances that *avoir* could take them into the past: *J'**ai** parlé avec Philip.* (I spoke to Philip.) Tu **as** mangé du poulet. (You ate *poulet.*)

And *avoir* having that kind of power did not sit well with *être* at all. To make it worse, *être* herself sometimes had to team up with *avoir himself to* form the *passé composé: Ils **ont été** très malades,* (They were very sick). ***J'ai été** très déçu,* (I was very disappointed.) *Vous **avez été** avec moi.* (You were with me). Things were pretty bad.

AVOIR and *ÊTRE* together in the *PASSÉ COMPOSÉ*

	PRONOUNCED	TRANSLATION
J'ai été	JAY- ETA	I was
Tu **as** été	AH- ETA	You were
Il, elle, on **a** été	AH- ETA	He, she, it, one was, or we were
Ils, elles **ont** été	ON- ETA	They were
Vous **avez** été	AV-A-ETA	You were (formal, or you plural)

But while *avoir* owns the rights to most of the verbs to bring them into the *passé composé,* 17 powerful verbs joined *Team Être.* Yes, 17 verbs that *avoir* wanted, joined up with his enemy, *être.* (Remember, *passé compose* just means the past COMPOSED of different elements. The name tells you what it is. Here it's composed of *avoir* and *être.*)

These are the famous *Être 17.* 17 all important verbs, mostly verbs of motion: *sortir, partir, venir, arriver rentrer, descendre,* (go out, leave, come to, arrive, re-enter, descend) all ran to *être's* court.. Plus you will even live or die with *être. Tu es né.* (You are born) *Tu es mort.* (You are dead.)

But that wasn't the worst for the feud. Among the celebrated *Être 17* was *avoir's* best friend the biker, renegade, vroom, vroom artist, *aller!* Yes, *aller* teamed up with *être* to step back into the past. *Je suis allé, tu es allé, vous êtes allé...* etc. (I had gone, you have gone, you had gone).

Using the word **ADVENT** down the left side, some of the *Être 17 Team* is highlighted. (Don't memorize this ADVENT code, or even write it in your notebook, *que tu aimes.* You'll see why soon.

Arriver - Partir
Descendre - Monter
Venir - Aller
Entrer - Sortir
Naître - Mourir
Tomber - Rester

Here's *être* in the present tense.

ÊTRE	PRONOUNCED	TRANSLATION
Je suis	SUI	I am
Tu es	EH	You are
Il, elle, on est	EH	He, she, it, one is, or we are
Ils, elles sont	SON	They are
Vous êtes	ET	You are (formal, or plural you)

Here's another look at the *Être 17*. Lots of people (severe grammar nerds) remember this group by the acronym of the DR & MRS VANDERTRAMP. The doc and his wife's name is written down the left on this chart in bold.

This list of 17 includes verbs from ER, IR and RE. (Don't worry, there's an easier way to learn this.)

Devenir – to become – *devenu*	*Vous êtes devenu*
Revenir – to come back – *revenu*	*Elles sont revenues*
Monter – to go up – *monté*	*Ils sont montés*
Rester – to stay – *resté*	*Je suis resté*
Sortir – to exit *sorti*	*Tu es sorti*
Venir – to come – *venu*	*Il est venu*
Aller – to go – *allé*	*Je suis allé*
Naître – to be born – *né*	*Tu es né*
Descendre, to descend, de*scendu*	*Il est descendu*
Entrer – to enter – *entré*	*Vous êtes entré*

Retourner – to return – *retourné*	*Elles sont retournées*
Tomber – to fall – *tombé*	*Il est tombé*
Rentrer – to re-enter – *rentré*	*Elle est rentrée*
Arriver – to arrive – *arrivé*	*Je suis arrivé*
Mourir – to die – *mort*	*Ils sont morts*
Partir – to leave – *parti*	*Vous êtes partis*

You don't have to memorize this list. Invite a few of the *Être 17* into French-ville. You'll get accustomed to hearing the words together. Soon *être* with *je* **suis** *allée* will sound very right, while accidently using *avoir* with *j'ai allée,* will sound very wrong.

You'll quickly develop an ear for French. Say *être* conjugations out loud whenever possible. (I've never memorized lists. I've learned what sounds right and what's *off.* And of course lots from hearing Julio's lyrics.)

While grammar geeks know all about the Dr. and Mrs. Vandertramp by heart (of course) there's an easier, more visual way to familiarize yourself with the *Être 17.*

Let's meet them where they live… now THIS you can write down. (The previous ways were for you to know about, in case you hear about ADVENT or DR & MRS VANDERPUMP.) But that's how others learn, we're rebelling against that – instead, welcome home. This is the easy way to learn…

Bienvenue to the House of Être…

Être's 17 roomies can do everything with *être* here. Review the previous list. From arriving at the house, to leaving the house… they can go in, and out, rest inside, go upstairs, downstairs, they can even *naître,* be born there, and unfortunately, *tomber,* fall down the stairs, and *mourir,* die there. *Être généralement* works with verbs of movement forming the *passé composé,* **all things you can do at home. Now that's the way to remember it!** *H*ere are a few examples:

Je **suis** sorti de la maison.	I left the house
Tu **es** arrivé à la maison	You arrived at the house
Il, elle, on **est** resté à la maison	He, she, it, one, we stayed at the house
Ils, elles **sont** retournés à la maison	They returned to the house
Vous êtes **parti** de la maison.	You left the house

There's no reflexive verbs in the chart above, but remember -- ALL reflexive verbs go with *être*. Remember that. All reflexive verbs are used with *être*. ALWAYS. *Je me suis habillé,* (I got myself dressed). *Tu t'es lavé* (You washed yourself.) *Elle s'est amusée.* (She enjoyed herself). Notice anything interesting about these three sentences? They all have the word: "self" in them. Myself, yourself, herself. Reflexive verbs really are that simple. We might say: He behaved himself. She dressed herself. We escorted ourselves into the movies. The reflexive is nothing more than that. We use it all the time in English. Don't let it bother you, it's not that difficult.

Back to *être*. As this is one of the most common and flexible verbs, this bad girl superhero turns up in lots of idiomatic expressions. Here's a list of top uses, but don't stress, like with our link word chart, pick a few you'll use now, and save the rest. *C'est cool.* (Right there, that's *être* hiding in plain sight, the EST in *C'EST is ÊTRE.)*

C'est ça	That's it!
C'est la vie	That's life
C'est à dire	That's to say
C'est à moi, c'est à toi	It's mine, it's yours
Il est	He is, it is
C'est le pied	It's great. Terrific!
C'est à dire	That means, that's to say
Je suis désolé	I'm sorry
C'est ne pas grave	Don't worry, no problem, no big deal
Ce n'est pas possible	No way! Not possible
Ce n'est pas vrai	Unbelieveable, not true
Est-ce que	Is it that…?

Est-ce que is a super important word set. This handy-dandy saying can turn *anything* into a question. It loosely means "is it that?" The dog is black, becomes a question by adding, *est-ce que. Est-ce que* the dog is black? (*Est-ce que le chien est noir?*) Like *il y a* (there is, there are) don't think of *est-ce que* it as 3 separate words, think of it as one bonded word set that's spelled funny and can turn anything into a question. *Est-ce que* that'll be okay with you? (In spoken French, as in English, the intonation of your voice will show when it's a question and *est-ce que* is not needed. A dog? A cat? The way you express the phrase, shows it's a question.)

Let's look at *être* in the future. Okay, she gets a little rebellious here. (Bet you've heard the song, *Que sera, sera. Whatever will be, will be*…That's *être* at work.)

FUTURE	TRANSLATION
Je ser**ai**	I will be
Tu ser**as**	You will be
Il, elle, on ser**a**	He, she, it, one, we will be
Ils, elles ser**ont**	They will be
Vous ser**ez**	You will be (formal, you plural)

Yep *être's* gone a bit crazy here again after calming down and taking a break in *l'imparfait.* I'm hoping by now you've learned the pronunciation of these endings. The consonants T and the Z of *seront* and *serez* are, as usual, both silent.

Remember, the **future** tense for ALL verbs, in ALL conjugations ends in AI, AS, A, ONT, EZ. Again, the future tense written in French is *FUTOR,* which has the famous O. (Wink, wink.) Here, in the FUTOR, the *ils* and *elles* drop their ENT entourage and show up with ONT. Remember, FUTOR, in our world = **ONT**.

You'll just have to memorize *être* in the future tense. You'll be using *être* all the time. And soon it'll just sound right to you.

Here's *être* in 4.5 tenses

PRESENT	IMPARFAIT	PASSÉ COMPOSÉ	FUTURE
Je suis	J'étais	J'ai été	Je serai
Tu es	Tu étais	Tu as été	Tu seras
Il, elle, on est	Il, elle, on Était	Il, elle, on a été	Il, elle, on sera
Ils, elles sont	Ils, elles étaient	Ils, elles ont été	Ils, elles seront
Vous êtes	Vous étiez	Vous avez été	Vous serez

And of course, *EN TRAIN DE* coming in here at one half a point. Making it the 4.5 tenses (*Je suis **en train de** partir de la maison.*) *Touché*!

By now you're accustomed to the big time ER verbs, flashy bad boys, and the one superhero bad girl, *être*, with her own train. But here we'll be joining more IR verbs. It's the second largest group of verbs but not even close to the massive size of the ER family. This is *avoir's* family. A very different camp of verbs – but lucky for us -- the IR group raided ER territory, stole a bunch of their formatting ideas and snuck off in the night.

Yes, lucky for us, because the IR family stole tons of patterns and configurations that we've already learned from the ER family. We're totally *in* with these IR dudes. WE. GOT. THIS.

Here's just some of what you'll recognize: *Vous* is here with his EZ security blanket. The ENT endings are back with *ils* and *elles*. (They'll switch to ONT of course, with the future, or FUTOR tense.) Our buddy Stu is here, (*tu* toting around his S). *Je* and *tu* often end in S – while *il, elle* and *on* often end in T. (Remember S comes before T in the alphabets, so *je* and *tu* get S while next down the chart, the T goes with *il, elle, on*.) In *l'imparfait* everything is pronounced just like the word, *l'imparfait*, and the Kumbaya family has brought over lots of their matching sounds.

Don't worry if you're zoning out right now. It'll all come together. And again, take what you need and save the rest for future studies. Don't get burned out.

Below are three *regular* IR verbs conjugated. They all follow the same pattern, get to know one, two, or three, and you'll know them all. Notice below how the regular verbs in IR are overloaded with the letter S. (Think IRS.) IR also has some heavy weight irregular verbs that you must know, but only a few, still to come. (Luckily for us, the 1,000 easy-to-learn ER verbs and not the S heavy IR verbs, have taken over the French world.

CHOISIR (To choose)

PRESENT	IMPARFAIT	PASSÉ COMPOSÉ	FUTURE
	(Was/were /used to)	(Had)	(Will)
Je choisis	Je choisissais	J'ai choisi	Je choisirai
Tu choisis	Tu choisissais	Tu as choisi	Tu choisiras
Il, elle, on choisit	Il, elle, on choisissait	Il, elle, on a choisi	Il, elle, on choisira
Ils, elles choisissent	Ils, elles choisissaient	Ils, elles ont choisi	Ils, elles choisiront
Vous choisissez	Vous choisissiez	Vous avez choisi	Vous choisi-rez

FINIR (To finish)

Je finis	Je finissais	J'ai fini	Je finirai
Tu finis	Tu finissais	Tu as fini	Tu finiras
Il, elle, on finit	Il, elle, on finissait	Il, elle, on a fini	Il, elle, on finira
Ils, elles finissent	Ils, elles finissaient	Ils, elles ont fini	Ils, elles finiront
Vous finissez	Vous finissiez	Vous avez fini	Vous finirez

REMPLIR (To fill)

Je remplis	Je remplissais	J'ai rempli	Je remplirai
Tu remplis	Tu remplissais	Tu as rempli	Tu rempliras
Il, elle, on remplit	Il, elle, on remplissait	Il, elle, on a rempli	Il, elle remplira
Ils, elles remplissent	Ils, elles remplissaient	Ils, elles ont rempli	Ils, elles rempliront
Vous remplissez	Vous remplissiez	Vous avez rempli	Vous remplirez

What's happened to our seven member Kumbaya family, from *je* to *elles*? Will they show up here to help us with same sound pronunciation? Will the French Academy think of us and do a letter drop? YES! Kind of. Let's look at *choisir* again, in the present and *imparfait*.

		PRONOUNCED
PRESENT	IMPARFAIT	KUMBAYA 7 / VOUS
Je choisis	Je choisissais	CHOISI/CHOISSIS-A
Tu choisis	Tu choisissais	CHOISI/CHOISSIS-A
Il, elle, on choisit	Il, elle, on choisissait	CHOISI/CHOISSIS-A
Ils, elles choisissent	ils, elles choisissaient	CHOISSIS/CHOISSIS-A
Vous choisissez	Vous choisissiez	CHOISSI-A/CHOISS-IA

Notice the pronunciations in the *choisir* chart. The Kumbaya family is almost intact, all sounding the same, and *vous*, as usual, is pronounced a bit differently. But notice the one hiccup here? While the Kumbaya family is sticking together, their *ils* and *elles* have gone off the deep end in the present tense pronunciation. *Choisis*! There's an extra S sound added at the end. In all of the conjugations for regular IR verbs, the *ils* and *elles* will always deviate from the pack and add this S sound. (Hmmm, *ils* and *elles* even both have an S on them. Just saying...)

106

Why do we care? Because what you see is not what you get when it comes to pronunciation. When watching Netflix with French subtitles, or reading books and articles (about fascinating subjects, of course) you'll know how the words are pronounced. In the regular IR verbs, the Kumbaya family has the same sound in the present tense, and *imparfait* except for the little S heard on the *ils* and *elles*. Listen for the extra S.

Here are a few more common REGULAR IR verbs you can plug into this template whenever you're ready. You'll find them all to be S crazy, just like *choisir, remplir* and *finir* above.

BÂTIR (To build)
GROSSIR (To gain weight)
GRANDIR (To grow up)
RÉFLÉCHIR (To reflect upon)
RÉUSSIR (To succeed)
VIEILLIR (To get old)
CONVERTIR (To convert)
DÉFINIR (To define)
INVESTIR (To invest)
ÉTABLIR (To establish)
AGIR (To act)
ACCOMPLIR (To accomplish)

When conjugated, all will have exactly the same endings as those IR verbs above. And yes, they all have a heavy dose of the letter S. (Choisissaient, remplissais, finissait.) Remember – IRS.

The IR family may be smaller than the ER verb conglomerate, but they're no slouches. There are several irregulars -- crazy bad boys you'll need to know ASAP to converse in French. As usual, these irregulars will all beat to their own *tambours* and although they also end in IR they have little family re-semblance to the conjugated IR regular verbs above.

Here they are. Uber-important. Try to learn one-a-day. Take them on a jaunt to Frenchville, find them and circle them in the French book you're reading, pick them out of a magazine, have fun with these bad boys.

VOIR (To see)
COURIR (To run)
DEVOIR (To be able, should, must)
SERVIR (To serve)
DORMIR (To sleep)
MENTIR (To lie)
SORTIR (To go out)
PARTIR (To leave)
SENTIR (To feel)
VENIR (To come)
TENIR (To hold)
FALLOIR (Must do, should)

From this last verb *falloir* comes an expression that you'll hear constantly in French conversations. *Il **faut** que. Il **faut** que. Il **faut** que.* IT'S SO IMPORTANT. It's like us saying "you gotta, he must, we should, it's necessary, we ought to, you wanna?.... It's the SHOULD. MUST. HAD BETTER. OUGHT TO. IT'S NECESSARY TO, expression. *Il faut que tu apprennes cette expression*! (You must... should... ought to... had better... learn this expression, you'll hear it non-stop, and be using it all the time.) You will hear it 100 times a day. Not kidding.

Let's meet the irregular IR verbs *vouloir* and *pouvoir* together since they share some of the same traits. The Kumbaya family with its same sounds, is trying hard to work *ensemble*, but alas, these are all renegade verbs, so it's a bit tough for the seven family members to hold it all together here.

PRESENT TENSE	PRESENT TENSE	PRONOUNCED
VOULOIR (To want)	POUVOIR (To be able to, can)	
Je veux	Je peux	VEU/PEU
Tu veux	Tu peux	VEU/PEU
Il, elle, on veut	Il, elle, on peut	VEU/PEU
Ils, elles veulent	Ils, elles peuvent	VEUL/PEUV
Vous voulez	Vous pouvez	VOUL-A/POUV-A

Vouloir and *pouvoir* are not an exact match when conjugated, but we know how out-of-control verbs can get so it's not a bad team up.

IMPARFAIT	IMPARFAIT	PRONOUNCED
VOULOIR	POUVOIR	
Je voulais	Je pouvais	VOUL-A/POUV-A
Tu voulais	Tu pouvais	VOUL-A/POUV-A
Il, elle, on voulais	Il, elle, on pouvait	VOUL-A/POUV-A
Ils, elles voulaient	Ils, elles pouvaient	VOUL-A/POUV-A
Vous vouliez	Vous pouviez	VOUL-IA/POUV-IA

PASSÉ COMPOSÉ	PASSÉ COMPOSÉ
VOULOIR	POUVOIR
J'ai voulu	J'ai pu
Tu as voulu	Tu as pu
Il, elle, on a voulu	Il, elle, on pu
Ils, elles ont voulu	Ils, elles pu
Vous avez voulu	Vous avez pu

Here are two more irregular IR verbs that have a lot on common when conjugated. *Venir* and *tenir*. These are easy to learn together. But watch out, *être* is coming to steal the show in *venir's passé composé*. It's *être* NOT *avoir* who's needed there. (Remember we learned that *être* often works with verbs of movement? She's got those 17 roommates running all over her house.

Venir (to come) fits the bill perfectly to join the royal *être* club while *tenir* (to hold) is left in the cold outside her house and runs off using *avoir*.

PRESENT	PRESENT	PRONOUNCED
VENIR (To come)	TENIR (To hold)	
Je viens	Je tiens	VIEN/TIEN
Tu viens	Tu tiens	VIEN/TIEN
Il, elle, on vient	Il, elle, on tient	VIEN/TIEN
Ils, elles viennent	Ils, elles tiennent	VIEN/TIEN
Vous venez	Vous tenez	VIEN-A/TIEN-A

IMPARFAIT	IMPARFAIT	PRONOUNCED
Je venais	Je tenais	VEN-A/TEN-A
Tu venais	Tu tenais	VEN-A/TEN-A
Il, elle, on venait	Il, elle, on tenait	VEN-A/TEN-A
Ils, elles venaient	Ils, elles venaient	VEN-A/TEN-A
Vous veniez	Vous teniez	VEN-IA/TEN-IA

PASSÉ COMPOSÉ (ETRE)	PASSÉ COMPOSÉ (AVOIR)
Je suis venu	J'ai tenu
Tu es venu	Tu as tenu
Il, elle, on est venu	Il, elle, on tenu
Ils, elles sont venu	Ils, elles ont tenu
Vous êtes venu	Vous avez tenu

FUTURE	FUTURE
Je viendrai	Je tiendrai
Tu viendras	Tu tiendras
Il, elle, on viendra	Il, elle, on tiendra
Ils, elles viendront	Ils, elles tiendront
Vous viendrez	Vous tiendrez

(You can pronounce these few above without my help. As usual the S, T and Z aren't heard.)

Venir has its own special way of communicating. If you say VENIR DE, that means "just" as in just finished, just came from.... *Je viens de manger* (I **just** ate). *Tu viens de skier.* (You **were just** skiing.) *Ils vient de manger et skier.* (They **were just** eating and skiing.) Watch for this as you read, speak, watch films. Circle this every time you see it in a book you're reading. You'll see it often in French. *Venir de* is SUPER used all day and very important.

Hey, I'm on a roll now with this side-by-side verb view. Here are two more IR verbs side-by-side. *Partir and sortir.* These are two verbs that often get confused. People say *sortir* (to go out) when they mean partir and then say *partir* (to leave) when they mean *sortir.* Here's the key to getting this correct... it's a simple letter O. *Sortir* has the O and O stands for OUT.

The key word or concept with *sortir* is OUT. I'm going OUT tonight. He's getting OUT of the water now. She's getting the car OUT of the garage. Did you take the garbage OUT? Did you take your shoes OUT of the room? *Sortir* in the *passé composé* can go with *être* OR *avoir* depending on the use.

Tu es sortie de l'ecole (Did you get OUT of school?) Or *vous avez sorti les valises*? (Have you gotten the luggage OUT?)

Partir is to leave (the opposite of *arriver*). They're leaving from Madrid. I'm leaving Monday. She already left for home. *Partir* is usually movement on a much grander scale than *sortir.* You might *sortir* from the shower, but you will *partir* from Paris to New York. Just remember the O in SORTIR, it's the one that just means OUT.

As you can see with most of our side-by-side verbs, the Kumbaya family is really coming through for us, both in the present tense and *l'imparfait.*

SORTIR, PRESENT	PARTIR	PRONOUNCED
Je sors	Je pars	SOR/PAR
Tu sors	Tu pars	SOR/PAR
Il, elle, on sort	Il, elle, on part	SOR/PAR
Ils, elles sortent	Ils, elles partent	SOR/PAR
Vous sortez	Vous partez	SORT-A/PART-A

SORTIR, IMPARFAIT	PARTIR, IMPARFAIT	PRONOUNCED
Je sortais	Je partais	SORT-A/PART-A
Tu sortais	Tu partais	SORT-A/PART-A
Il, elle, on sortait	Il, elle, on partait	SORT-A/PART-A
Ils, elles sortaient	Ils, elles partaient	SORT-A/PART-A
Vous êtes sortiez	Vous avez partiez	SORT-IA/PART-IA

SORTIR, PASSÉ COMPOSÉ (Être and avoir at use here)	PARTIR, PASSÉ COMPOSÉ
Je suis; j'ai sorti	Je suis parti
Tu es; tu as sorti	Tu es parti
Il, elle, on est sorti; a sorti	Il, elle, on est parti
Ils, elles sont sortis; ont sortis	Ils, elles sont partis
Vous êtes; *vous* avez sorti	Vous êtes parti

SORTIR, FUTURE	PARTIR, FUTURE
Je sortirai	Je partirai
Tu sortiras	Tu partiras
Il, elle, on sortira	Il, elle, on partira
Ils, elles sortiront	Ils, elles partiront
Vous sortirez	Vous partirez

PART THREE

The RE Verbs,
the Geneva Convention,
and
a Know-it-All
Meets a Know-it-All

Three

I'm getting bored. Sorry, I am. My mind is floating in letter debris; I'm drowning in verb endings and spellings. I'm sure you're feeling the same.

But hold on. We're getting to the end. Yes, there is an end to all this madness. Just a little longer then we'll get to the fun stuff. Soon to come is...

LE SUPER COOL CHEAT SHEET,
PLUS
FUN BONUS MATERIAL,
RANDOM THOUGHTS,
FRENCH DOs AND DON'Ts,
CULTURAL POINTS,
ASSORTED INFO,
AND...
ARE YOU A PEACH
OR A COCONUT?

Yes, that's the next section. Meanwhile, let's finish the IR verbs and deal with the smallest group, the RE verbs.

I'm keeping this short because -- I gotta tell you -- this verb study is killing me. I know, I know, you're not in love with it either. But, you think it's hard on you? Hey, I'm writing all this, I REALLY have to be on top of it. OMG! I'm even dreaming about this now. Yikes!

Last night I had a nightmare about the RE verb, *connaître*. I was at the Geneva convention. The Geneva verb convention. The room was packed, there was a big ol' bald master of ceremonies. He grabbed a mic as he waddled back-and-forth over the stage:

MC: Ladies and Gentleverbs, welcome to the 47th annual Geneva Convention. We've got some very high-profile guests here tonight.

Among our 14 illustrious panel members, we have *Aller*, to talk about going places.

Manger is here to talk about French cuisine; *Danser* will demonstrate new tango steps, and of course, *Savoir* is here to talk about everything because, as we all know, *Savior* knows everything! In addition, we have...

A male verb dressed in a dark blue suit with a red tie jumped up in the audience.

CONNAÎTRE: Stop! Stop right here! *Savoir* does not know everything! I'm the verb TO KNOW. I know everything!

MC: Sir, you there -- please can you sit down. Sir!

CONNAÎTRE: NO! I will not! I know far more than *savoir*! He's a phony, a fraud! Get him off the stage!

MC: Security, remove this verb!

The elegant *Savoir* springs from his seat on stage.

SAVOIR: Yes, remove him! I am the great *savoir*. I know *everything* -- he knows nothing!

115

CONNAÎTRE: Ha! I know everybody and every place on earth. I KNOW PRINCE HARRY!

MC: Security, remove this out-of-control verb at once.

SAVOIR: You may have met Prince Harry...

CONNAÎTRE: And Lady Gaga..

SAVOIR: ... but I KNOW how to become King! I KNOW how to dress like royalty, and I KNOW how to send you to the galleons. And I will!

CONNAÎTRE: Oh? Really? I am the real, authentic verb: TO KNOW. You're nothing without some random verb nearby. If there isn't a verb in the same sentence with you – you don't exist.

SAVOIR: Je *sais* danser. Je *sais* voyager. Je *sais* manger. Je *sais* jouer au tennis. Je *sais faire tout. Tout!* I KNOW! I KNOW1 I KNOW!

CONNAÎTRE: So what – maybe you DO know how to dance, to travel, to eat, and to play tennis. For you to know anything there must be a verb around. You just had to add *danser, voyager, manger, jouer.* Me, I work alone! If there is NO verb in a sentence – then I'm still *knowledgeable*.

SAVOIR: Oh? Really? I am the verb: TO KNOW! You can't do anything without reference to a person or place, an item, a monument, a building, a statue, you don't actually *know* how to DO anything! You may know people and places, but I know how to DO everything!

CONNAÎTRE: *Huh ! Big deal! Je connais tout le monde.* I know the whole world. *Je connais Paris, Morroco, Rio.* I know Paris, Morroco, Rio. *Je connais Beyonce and Jay-Z.* Yes, I know Beyonce and Jay-Z. *Je connais Ariana Grande et Miley Cyrus. Je connais les Champs Élysée, le Grand Canyon, la Statue de la Liberté.* And that's just a few of the places and people I know. I know everyone and everywhere.

SAVOIR: Braggart! You're just a braggart, a name dropping, destination dropping oaf! That's all you know! People and places.

The pudgy master of ceremonies raises his microphone shouting…

MC: Security – remove *connaître* at once! *Savoir* means TO KNOW! He's our panel expert.

SECURITY: Both mean to know. *Connaître* knows everyone and every place. *Savoir* knows how *to do* everything. But my buddy *connaître* doesn't need a verb. If there's a proper name, a person, an item, a monument, or destination, anything with *no verb* around—then *connaître* is your guy.

MC: That's crazy talk. To know is to know, know what I mean?

SECURITY: Like if you say, *je **connais** filet mignon.* It means I know, or I am familiar with, *filet mignon.* You've heard of it or been around it. But if there's a verb, or reference to a verb, then savoir is your man. *Je **sais** comment **faire** un filet mignon.* (**I know** how **to make** *filet mignon.*) Then it's *savoir's* territory. He KNOWS how to make it.

A thin, beautiful verb dressed in velvet, and carrying an oversized Louis Vuitton bag, rises up in the audience. She wears a diamond and emerald crown.

ÊTRE: Excuseeeee meeeee… Helloooooo!

MC: Now what? Miss, please sit down!

ÊTRE: Hi *Connaître*, I know Prince Harry too, we had our crowns made by the same royal jeweler in London.

Avoir is in the audience and bolts up out of his seat.

AVOIR: Sit down, *Être*! Your diamonds are surely fakes! Go back to your stupid House of *Être* and stay gone! HA! Both c*onnaître* and *savoir* work with ME not you and your silly little 17 roommates.

A nasty brawl erupted. The MC barely got out alive vowing never to deal with verbs again! (Verbs have way too many issues.)

What a nightmare! Dreaming about verbs is a nightmare for sure. Anyway, where was I? Let's finish up with just one IR verb. Might as well end with the know-it-all, *savoir*.

SAVOIR, PRESENT TENSE	PRONOUNCED
Je **sais**	SAI
Tu **sais**	SAI
Il, elle, on **sait**	SAI
Ils, elles **savent**	SAV
Vous sav**ez**	SAV-A

Look it over, you've been here before, it's not that unfamiliar. See the patterns? *Je* has the classic ai. (*je vais, j'ai, j'allais, je penserai*). *Tu* has the S, for Stu. (*Tu vas, T'as, Tu allais, tu manges*) *Je* and *tu* both have the final S, then next down is the T ending, for *il, elle, on*. S then T just like in the alphabet. (*Je, tu parlais, il, elle on parlait*) *Vous* has his EZ, and *ils* and *elles* have their ENT ending. In *l'imparfait* in all other verbs we studied, the endings were ais, ais, ait, aient, iez. Let's see how we do here when we drop not just the IR from savoir, but the whole OIR.

SAVOIR, L'IMPARFAIT

Je sav**ais**	SAV-A
Tu sav**ais**	SAV-A
Il, elle, on sav**ait**	SAV-A
Ils, elles sav**aient**	SAV-A
Vous sav**iez**	SAV-IA

Perfect. Like all bad boy verbs, *savoir* calms down in *l'imparfait* and uses a word closer to his stem. The endings here match all other verbs we've studied. Easy to remember. We've already reviewed this. Plus the Kumbaya family of same sounds is back in true form.

Here's the *passé composé* using *avoir* for a helping hand to get into the past.

SAVOIR, PASSÉ COMPOSÉ
J'**ai** su
T'**as** su
Il, elle, on **a** su
Ils, elles **ont** su
Vous **avez** su

SAVOIR, FUTURE
Je saur**ai**
Tu saur**as**
Il, elle, on saur**a**
Ils, elles saur**ont**
Vous saur**ez**

After their battle *royale*, do you understand the difference between the two know-it-alls? *Savoir* will always be siding with a verb. I know how *to dance*. I know how *to make* fondue. I know *to tie* slip knots. *Savoir* knows nothing unless there's a verb around. And it can be ANY verb. Or even *referencing a verb unseen*. For example, if you KNOW something by heart, then you *learned* it. *Apprendre* (to learn) is at play there, even though it is not seen or heard. *Je sais cette chanson par coeur*. Whenever *par coeur* is used (by heart) use SAVOIR.

Connaître means to be familiar with, to be acquainted with. *Je connais Luc. Je connais Miami, Je connais le Hip Hop*. (Jay-Z could say "*je SAIS Hip Hop*" since he wrote some of it, and knows much of it *par coeur*, or by heart.) If you can replace, *I'm familiar with* in sentences, and·you speak of places, people, monuments, towers, attractions… then you're with *connaître*.

Welcome to RE verbs, with *connaître* on crutches.

Connaître didn't do too well in the battle of Geneva. *Savoir* was always a much stronger verb and *knows how* to do all kinds of things! Savoir began the fight by doing everything he knew how to do, *c'était fou!* (It was crazy!)

He began throwing chairs, then playing air guitar, singing, doing tai chi, winking, aiming karate kicks, he was doing 100 different things that he knew how to do.

Meanwhile, *connaître* was doing what he knows best, calling for reinforcement from people he knows: officials, police, the SWAT team, Swiss bankers, his friends; He tried to reach Prince Harry.

Here's *connaître* in *le present* tense, *l'imparfait*, the *passé composé* and the *futor*. He's irregular, but not too bad.

PRESENT (To know, to be familiar with)
Je conn**ais**
Tu conn**ais**
Il, elle, on conn**aît**
Ils, elles conn**aissent**
Vous conn**aissez**

IMPARFAIT
Je conn**aissais**
Tu conn**aissais**
Il, elle, on conn**aissait**
Ils, elles conn**aissaient**
Vous conn**aissiez**

PASSÉ COMPOSÉ
J'**ai** connu
Tu **as** connu
Il, elle, on **a** connu
Ils, elles **ont** connu
Vous **avez** connu

Let's take a break, stop for a minute and look at a general overview of the *l'imparfait*. By now you've been acquainted with most of these following verbs. Here they are for the first time together. These are some ER, IER, IR, and RE verbs, both regular and irregular, side-by-side:

Pronoun	Ending	parler parl-	finir finiss-	étudier étudi-	manger mange-	être ét-	*connaître* *connaît*
Je (j')	**-ais**	parlais	finissais	étudiais	mangeais	étais	connaissais
Tu	**-ais**	parlais	finissais	étudiais	mangeais	étais	connaissais
Il, elle, on	**-ait**	parlait	finissait	étudiait	mangeait	était	connaissait
Ils, elles	**-aient**	parlaient	finissaient	étudiaient	mangeaient	étaient	Connais saient
Vous	**-iez**	parliez	finissiez	étudiiez	mangiez	étiez	connaissiez

If you have trouble remembering what the *l-imparfait* tense represents, it means the IMPERFECT tense. So it's an imperfect act, and comes from the Latin word *imperfectus*, which means unfinished. And that's what it represents. Things you were doing, something you had been doing, something you used to do. Example, I was walking. I used to walk. These are unfinished, imperfect acts. They are very different than saying: I WALKED.

Reminder: For all future tense regular ER endings we use the entire verb as the stem, the whole shebang, then add to it. (Aren't ER verbs great?) We've been adding the endings: ai, as, a, ont, ez. Regular RE verbs also follow this pattern: but first -- remove the just the final E from the RE ending of the infinitive and then add your future endings, just like *connaître*, below:

FUTURE
Je connait**rai**
Tu connait**ras**
Il, elle connait**ra**
Ils, elles connait**ront**
Vous connait**rez**

What's so special about RE verbs? Who exactly are they? We've gone through the powerhouses of some RE irregular verbs, *être* and *connaître*.

Now we can take a break and deal with some top REGULAR RE verbs that you'll use daily in French.

ATTENDRE: (To wait)
DÉFENDRE: (To defend)
DESCENDRE: (To descend)
ENTENDRE: (To hear)
ÉTENDRE: (To stretch)
FONDRE: (To melt)
PENDRE: (To hang, suspend)
PERDRE: (To lose)
PRÉTENDRE: (To claim)
RENDRE: (To give back)
RÉPANDRE: (To spread, scatter)
RÉPONDRE: (To answer)
VENDRE: (To sell)

Here's the present tense conjugation of regular RE verbs. Simple! Like all the regular ER and IR verbs the KUMBAYA family is here and well. Except for the *vous*, all the rest, from *JE* to *ELLES*, once again the entire 7 member Kumbaya family is all pronounced the same. While *vous* is ATTEND-A, PERD-A and VEND-A, all the rest are simply: ATTEND, PERD, VEND. Oops! I didn't mean to say that, I didn't mean to pronounce it for you – because – YOU. GOT. THIS. By now in our journey together, you know the good ol' Kumbaya family and how they work together. Here they are again, *ensemble,* making French pronunciation simple.

Pronoun		*Attendre*	*Perdre*	V*endre*
J'(or Je)	**-s**	attends	perds	vends
Tu	-s	attends	perds	vends
Il, elle	-	attend	perd	vend
Ils, elles, on	**-ent**	attendent	perdent	vendent
vous	**-ez**	attendez	perdez	vendez

Now here are our RE regular verbs in the *imparfait* and *passé composé*. Note I'm using *avoir* as the helping hand in the *passé composé*.

ATTENDRE, IMPARFAIT	VENDRE, IMPARFAIT	PRONOUNCED
J'attendais (to wait)	Je vendais (to sell)	ATTEND-A/VEND-A
Tu attendais	Tu vendais	ATTEND-A/VEND-A
Il, elle, on attendait	Il, elle, on vendait	ATTEND-A/VEND-A
Ils, elles attendaient	Ils, elles vendaient	ATTEND-IA/VEND-A
Vous attendiez	Vous vendiez	ATTEND-IA/ VEND-IA

ATTENDRE, PASSÉ COMPOSÉ	VENDRE, PASSÉ COMPOSÉ
J'ai attendu	J'ai vendu
Tu as attendu	Tu as vendu
Il, elle, on a attendu	Il, elle, on a vendu
Ils, elles ont attendu	Ils, elles ont vendu
Vous avez attendu	Vous avez vendu

Remember in the future tense (*FUTOR*) the ENT ending of *ils* and *elles*, is replaced with the ONT. The classic ENT ending is changed there. (*Avoir* and *être* also borrow an ONT, check out their conjugations and see where they use it.)

ATTENDRE, FUTURE	VENDRE, FUTURE
J'attendrai	Je vendrai
Tu attendras	Tu vendras
Il, elle, on attendra	Il, elle, on vendra
Ils, elles attendront	Ils, elles vendront
Vous attendrez	Vous vendrez

That's it. That's about all I've got for you. I do want you to look up *DIRE* (to say) and *FAIRE* (to do, or to make) two very irregular, and very important RE verbs. There are about 20 irregular RE verbs, so pick out a few you'll need the most, and search around the web.

It's time for you to do your own research, to take action, be proactive, and plant this growing list of verbs in your cerebrum.

It's been a pleasure to work with you. I hope I've helped you learn a bit of French, making it just a bit friendlier.

As a going away present, (of course I wasn't going to abandon you that easily), I'm giving you a cheat sheet with a bunch of fun random facts, from how much to tip in France – to how to survive there. We'll go on a word safari, check out a secret language, even pop open a bottle of bubbly. Stay tuned.

Don't forget to use your notebook, *que tu aimes*, and off we go. (Think of your notebook as your study buddy. It's the two of you together in this.) *Vive la Frenchville!*

LE SUPER COOL CHEAT SHEET

PLUS
FUN BONUS MATERIAL,
RANDOM THOUGHTS,
ASSORTED INFO,
FRENCH DOs AND DON'Ts,
CULTURAL POINTS,
AND...
ARE YOU A PEACH
OR A COCONUT?

Hold on. This is the best part of the book. Don't leave now...

This section is a mix of everything: find out if the French really wear berets; how much you should tip, and the best use for a safety pin. Plus, why there are so many pharmacies in France, why you should never place a *baguette* upside down, and the best kept secret about where to stay in Paris.

I didn't just gather up the main points of the book and repeat it all here. *Bof non*! This is a little gift. *Un cadeau pour toi.* This is the fun part. (Not that verb conjugation wasn't fun! Um, okay, to be honest – it wasn't. As you know by now, *je déteste ça.)*

But here I've got all the random bonus material – some things that we've covered in the book, just to remind you, plus things we haven't covered. Stay with me. If you don't read further, you'll miss all the interesting facts. Stick around.

Ready, set, here we go… in no special order…

The "other" French language.

Introducing the secret French language: *VERLAN*. You've got the know about *VERLAN* to be admitted into the oh-so-secret world of *français*.

Remember how I laughed about the French Academy? It's the real deal, a renowned institution in Paris, and they HATE when anyone plays around with French. There are some serious, big time, powerful bayonet slinging French dames and dudes there. They make the rules and the number one rule is to keep the French language – 100% French. Unlike English where new words are introduced constantly (selfie, butt-dial, ghosting, hangry, rando.) New words are rarely introduced into the official French language. It's simply un-French.

So what's a Frenchie to do? How can they play with their own language? How can they beat the French Academy? Voila! They invented *VERLAN*.

Verlan is the cool language that those 'in the know' speak. (Parents, bosses, and teachers are often not hip to this dialect). But don't worry, this isn't a whole new language you have to learn. A few words will get you up-to-date.

Verlan is a way of switching syllables around. The word *verlan* itself is the played with way of saying the French word, *l'envers*, (backwards). *Verlan* = *l'envers* = *vers-l'en*. Got it? Basically, the word is spun around and a bit chopped up, sometimes a U is added, or a letter is dropped, if it makes the word sound better.

Here are some of the top *verlan mots et expressions à retenir* (words and phrases to remember) – and you will often hear them by native French speakers.

Cimer	Merci, thank you
Ouf	Fou, crazy
Teuf	Fete, party
Reuf	Frère, brother
Meuf	Femme, woman
Reum	Mère, mother
Oim	Moi, me
Venere	Énervé, angry
Zarbi	Bizarre, bizarre
Chelou	Louche, shady character

More local jargon.

Let's stay with the local flair. Here are some more great words to add to your notebook, *que tu aimes*, as they're used a lot in French.

Kiffe. This is slang for aimer (to like/to love). Today everybody "*kiffes*" things.

Je le kiffe, I love it.
Je kiffe les bananes, I love bananas.

Est-ce que tu kiffe? Are you happy? (Remember we learned *est-ce que*? It's the verb *être* turning anything into a question.)

C'est top! Means it's the best, cool. And yes, again, the French do say our word COOL a lot.

OMG! The French don't have their own way of saying OMG! They use ours. Yes, LOL and OMG are often used by the French, lifted from English. But they do have lots of their own shortcuts for texting and emails...

SVP, STP	S'il vous plait, s'il te plait, please
MDR	Mort de rire, dying of laughter, equivalent to our LOL.
QDN	Quoi de neuf, what's new?
QQ1,	Quelqu'un, someone
PK	Pourquoi, why
BIZ	Bisous, bises, kisses
DSL	Desolé, sorry
DAC	D'accord, agreed, ok, alright
ENTK	En tout cas, anyway, in any case
CHUIS	Je suis, I am

Speaking of using *chui*s, as *je suis* written above. The pronunciation of *je suis* is spoken all day long as just *CHUIS* (shh-we). In fast spoken French, as in English, lots of letters are eaten. *Je suis* becomes simply *CHUIS* (shh-we). You'll hear that MORE than you'll hear *je suis*. Just *CHUIS*!

Tu as (you have) is shortened to *t'a*. *T'a mon livre*? (Do you have my book?) This is in fast spoken French only, maybe for written texts or Facebook posts. Otherwise we know that it is practically illegal in the French language to contract *TU*.

Chui (je suis) certaine que t'a (tu as) mon livre. (I'm sure that you have my book.)

Berets and French Navy Shirts.

Let's move to clothing. Does anyone *really* wear berets and those famous French blue and white striped shirts, *le marinière,* in France?

Heck yeh! Berets will be worn when it's cool out, but in darker colors, like black or navy. Only tourists wear red berets... with blue and white striped shirts. (This is a neon sign for every pickpocket in Paris to rob you.) You do not want to look like a tourist. That means, no Disney T-shirts (unless you're at Disney Paris). No over-sized hoodies and hiking boots, or big oversized sneakers. No backwards baseball caps with over-sized t-shirts. The French always wear clothes that fit them, go figure.

You don't want to dress in leggings or sweats like you're headed to the gym. That's an obvious tourist uniform. Wear what you like, of course, but you don't want to become a metro robbery victim. (I travel with a simple safety or diaper pin. I'll stuff my daily ration of cash and cards in my front pocket and lock it in with a 10-cent pin. No pick pocket in the world has ever been able to rob me. I was recently on a packed metro in Barcelona, and everyone around me was robbed by a herd of pickpockets, They're great at knocking into you and at the same time stealing everything. Fully stuffed wallets were lifted from pockets and handbags all around me when passengers were "accidently" shoved. My simple pin saved me, again.)

Now, let's get to the famous, classic, sexy Breton blue and white striped shirts. Here's the deal... In 1858 these striped shirts were adopted as part of the French navy uniform. It had 20 white stripes (20 mm, or 0.79 inches wide) and 21 blue stripes (10 mm, or 0.39 inches wide). The sleeves were to have no more than 15 white and 15 blue stripes. In 1913 Coco Chanel began wearing these shirts as standard fare on her seaside vacations, and a new iconic look was born.

Among many, James Dean, John Wayne, Pablo Picasso, Brigitte Bardot and Jean Paul Gaultier have all been photographed in these famous French shirts. They're still made today at the original factory in Normandy, France, by the company St James. (Check them out: Saint-James.com)

Coco Chanel at her seaside retreat, in her classic stripped shirt.

Are you a peach or a coconut?

The French are thought to be real snobs, especially wait-staff. The French government went as far as launching two multi-million-dollar ad campaigns to teach them to treat tourists better. But the French are just different from other cultures. The French, Russians, and Germans are cultural coconuts. While Americans, Brazilians and the Japanese are considered to be peaches.

From the book, *The Culture Map*, by Erin Meyer:

In peach cultures, such as the United States, people are more likely to be open and friendly ("soft") with those they just met. In this type of culture, people tend to smile more frequently at strangers, share information about themselves, and ask personal questions of others. However, once you get past the initial pleasantries the hard shell of the pit may stop you, which is where the peach protects its real self.

In contrast, in a coconut culture, such as France, people tend to be more closed off ("hard") with people that they do not already have a relationship with. In this type of culture, people rarely smile at strangers or share info with those they do not know. It may take longer to warm up to someone in this culture, but after breaking through the outer shell, the relationship will become more open and fluid.

While the French aren't overly polite and open to strangers, Americans are known to be *too* open, bubbly and forward with new people. Americans are smiley and chatty on the surface, but this initial openness is often stopped once others get too close. There's a wall, a pit under the surface, preventing newcomers from entering. For this reason, Americans are often thought to be phony, deceptive, and superficial by other cultures.

French are more like coconuts. Hard shelled. They won't reveal themselves, or give too much information to strangers. They may not smile and can be very suspicious if you're too open with them, too quickly. It takes time to get to know them, time for them to reveal their interior. For this reason, French are considered to be cold, brusk, and rude by other cultures.

Are you a peach or a coconut? It seems like a mixture of the two would be best.

A nasty divorce.

Here's a great trick you need to know. It'll make your life so much easier. The famous French *NE...PAS* partnership has broken up. *Ne* and *pas* have gone their own ways. Divorced! And that's great news for us.

Here's what I mean... to say the negative in French you had to first use NE, then add PAS.

Like this:

BEFORE	MEANING	AFTER THE DIVORCE
Je **ne** sais **pas.**	I don't know	Je sais **pas**
Tu **ne** danses **pas.**	You don't dance	Tu dance **pas**
Vous **n'**écoutez pas	You don't listen	Vous écoutez **pas**

Before *ne* and *pas* always worked as a team. But now in informal spoken French everybody drops the *ne*, (Bye *ne*,) and *pas* works alone, (Hello *pas*).

(Notice the *N'ecoutez* above? Remember? It would have been *NE écoutez*, but we dropped the E of the NE, replacing it with an apostrophe, to help pronunciation.)

Also, take a look above at the *Je ne sais pas*. We had dropped the *ne* and it became *je sais pas*. In spoken French this will be shortened again. It is said as JE PAS, dropping even the verb *savoir (je sais),* and will now be pronounced *jepas (Chupa or shh pa).* Thus *je ne sais pas = je sais pas = je pas* = pronounced *chupa.*) So now with a shrug of your shoulders and a *chupa*, you can say you don't know. Hold on to this one. You'll really sound French.

Getting around *arrondissments.*

If you know all about Paris, or, for that matter, anything I've spoken about in this book, please excuse these little info splashes. For the rest, this is about the distinct areas in Paris. It's easy to move around from section to section and get to know their personalities. Paris is actually a small town.

Ask someone where they live in Paris and they might say, the 4th, or the 7^{th,} or another number up to 20. These little cities, or *arrondissments* start in the middle with numbers 1 and 2, and swirl outward, like the colorful lollipop. That's why the 7th for example, is next to both the 1st, and 16th as you can see by the map.

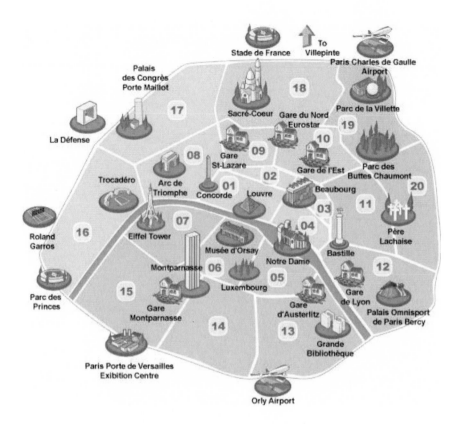

What is an *arrondissment*, anyway? Called the '20 little cities,' the *arrondissments* are *barrios*, or districts, each has its own mayor and town hall. (*Quartiers* are older neighborhoods in Paris). These districts were numbered back in the 1860's, during the rebuilding of Paris, by Baron Haussmann. (He was Napoleon Bonaparte's nephew. A fascinating story in itself). The 1st and 2nd *arrondissments* are the heart of Paris, the smallest, oldest, and among the most beloved. These were the seat of royal power in France's history.

The 3rd and 4th are called *les marais*, the marshes, built on swampland. It was favored by aristocracy from the 13th to 17th centuries.

The chic 5th and 6th, lay on *La Rive Gauche*, (the Left Bank of the river Seine.) This is the Latin *quartier* and *Saint-Germain-des-Prés.*" Centuries ago, scholars from the nearby Sorbonne University wandered these same cobblestone streets, speaking Latin, hence the name *Quartier Latin.*

This is what medieval Paris looked like. (These quaint districts were spared the sweeping Paris renovations of Haussmann.) In the 6th, on the wall of Shakespeare and Company, a bohemian bookstore hangout, is one of my favorite quotes: "Be not inhospitable to strangers, lest they be angels in disguise." (Look for the famous cat lounging around the store).

The 7th is the *Tour Eiffel.* (Here's where you can safely wear your beret to get a selfie with the *Tour* in the background.)

Every *arrondissment,* as you swirl out from the quaint center, clockwise towards the 2 airports and outlaying highways, has unique features and attractions. Each one is a *cité* onto itself. Each worth exploring.

I often stayed in the 14th, and here's why… (It's also the best kept secret in Paris for students and young adventurers). The 14th has the *Cité Internationale Universitaire.* Yes, the City University. This huge international campus empties out in the summer. Students either graduate, or return home for a break to Saudi Arabia, Africa, South America, etc. Their rooms are empty! Empty rooms – in Paris – on a beautiful, park-like campus -- and the cafeteria and library are open. Get it!?!

Every summer for years I'd go to Paris and grab a dorm room. It was $5.00 a night. (Paid to the security guards.) A safe, clean, centrally located, garden and park-filled campus, $5.00 a night in Paris! And the cafeteria was serving great food. Few people knew about this. I was told by a fellow traveler when I was in my early 20's. It was the perfect hangout for twenty-something summers in Paris. Hmmm, I might have to do it again.

(Btw: The word *collège* in French does not mean college, or university, it means middle school, or Jr high school.)

Um, huh, so, like, ya know, ah, whatever…

Here are a few interjections, or filler words you'll hear thrown into French sentences. (These are equivalent to our English fillers: Um, huh, so, like, ah, ya know.)

BLING	Pronounced	Meaning	Use
Bref	Bref	In short	Bref j'ai mangé trop. (In short, I ate too much)
Bof	Bo	Dunno	Tu aimes ça? (You like it?) Bof. (It's ok)
Ouais	Ouway	Oui	Tu veux ca ? (You want that ?) Ouais. (Oui)
Hein	EI .	Right	J'ai l'air bien, hein? (I look good, right)
En fait	En fet	Actually	En fait, je l'aime lui. (Actually I like him.)
Genre	Gen	Like	Donc, genre quand? (So like when?)
Euh	Au	Umm	Euh, je sais pas. (Umm, I don't know)
Ah bah Oui	Ah ba we	Okay, yes	Ah bah oui on y va. (Okay, let's go)
Là	Là	Right now	Tu fait quoi, là? (What are you doing now?)
Quoi	Qua	You know	C'est drôle, quoi (It's funny, you know)
Tu sais	Tu say	You know	C'est drôle, tu sais (It's funny, you know)

You're so rude.

How to be polite in France? *Don't be on time*. The French have the well-used expression *"les 15 minutes de politesse."* The 15 minutes of politeness. When you're invited to someone's house, make sure you're 15 minutes late to give them extra time to prepare. (Not more time, or you'll be considered to be rude; not less time, or you'll be considered to be rude. Just 15 minutes.) And ALWAYS bring a gift, even if the host insists she doesn't need anything. Flowers, a decent wine, or chocolates are always a good choice.

When bringing flowers make sure you bring an odd number. 7, 9, 11, 15 (not 13) it's unlucky to bring an even number. Tell the florist these are *pour offrir*, (a gift) so he'll know the other rules, like not to give you chrysanthemums, (for gravesites), red carnations, (ill-will), red roses (only for lovers), yellow flowers (unfaithfulness). All white flowers are for (weddings only). Phew... let the florist or flower market seller figure it out.

Speaking of rude, always start a greeting with *bonjour*... or *bonsoir* (after 6pm). These are expected, ALWAYS. As Americans we don't walk around saying 'Good day'. It's not a habit here. But it's *a must* in France. Think of it as saying 'hello,' and 'excuse me,' and 'how are you', all at once.

You may think that you're being polite if you step up to a stranger and say, 'Excuse me, is this the way to the *tour Eiffel*?' But no, in France – even that's extremely rude. You must first say '*Bonjour, Madame,* (or *Monsieur*) first, then -- is this the way to the *tour Eiffel*.' *Bonjour* is the magic word. ALWAYS. If you're in a store, restaurant, pharmacy -- step up to the counter and say *bonjour* first. (There was a book written about this called *The Bonjour Effect. The Secret Codes of French Conversation*.)

Greetings are offered with a light handshake. Kissing on both cheeks or *"faire la bise"* is the greeting among family, friends and colleagues. You're not really kissing, your lips don't touch skin. As you know, these are air kisses, first to the left cheek, then right. Never hug a French person. While 'kissing' is fine, hugging is a no-no, it's too much of an invasion of personal space. Just don't.

Why so many pharmacies? And the best one in Paris.

Every year during Paris Fashion week, you can't get into the *Cité* Pharmacy in the 6th, *Saint Germain*. It's packed with every model and stylist from all over the world. This is THE pharmacy to go to in Paris. They have every skincare and beauty product you could imagine all *at half* what you'd pay outside of France. This is a must-do in Paris. (By 10 am every day, yearlong, it can be so crowded, it's hard to move around.)

You'll notice there are about 3 pharmacies on every block in Paris. What's up with that? The French are the known as the biggest Rx poppers in Europe. Go to a doctor with a simple cold and you will get 4 prescriptions. It's the culture. And it's all free for them.

Oh, and speaking of shopping, do you know what window shopping is called in France? Window licking. *Lèche-vitrine*, as in *j'aime faire du lèche-vitrine*. Je l'aime. (I love to lick windows.... aka window shopping.) Window lickers is a derogatory term for the mentally handicapped in the UK.

Back to grammar for a sec.

Here's a chart for our present tense regular verb endings. *Nous* is back in the mix so you can get familiar with it as you'll see it in written form, but not usually spoken. You'll see that a conjugated *NOUS* uses the letters ONS. 3 letters found in the word *NOUS* itself!

REGULAR **PRESENT TENSE**

	-ER	-IR	-RE
Je	e	is	s
Tu	es	is	s
Il/Elle/On	e	it	
Nous	ons	issons	ons
Vous	ez	issez	ez
Ils/Elles	ent	issent	ent

A bit more grammar.

Two French verbs mean to bring: *Apporter* and *amener*. One means to bring an inanimate object: *I'll bring wine to the party.* And one means to bring a person or animal. *I'm also bringing my pet pigs to the party.* Looking at the two words. Can you figure out which is which? Hint, the answer is written right in the words. Do you see it?

Okay -- *amener* has the word MEN in it. Yep, that's the one used to bring people or animals. Apporter has the word PORT in it. Think port wines. So an object is right in the word. (Don't ask me why I always see these things.)

The French Zoo

There's lots of Zoomorphic use in France. (Zoo-morphing. Yes, that's a word. English, of course.) People are commonly, affectionately called by animal and insect names, especially kids or significant others... My hen, my island canary, my rabbit, my flea, (yes calling your lover "my flea," *ma puce*, is very, very common) my ant, kitten, wolf, and dove. These are used ALL THE TIME.

Food, glorious food.

France is a food nation. Life is built around it. Here are a few facts about food there.

The French bread, *baguette* will be laid on the table and pieces ripped off. Often no bread plate is used you just put the bread back on the table as you eat it. (An odd custom for Americans). Never lay the *baguette* upside down on the table, top up always, or it's bad luck.

Dinner in France is usually around 8 or 9 pm. Most French will only eat 3 times a day, snacking is not usual. 3 full meals, and a possible 4pm "*gouter*." This is the classic snack time that kids come home to everyday after school. Adults will sometimes have a *gouter* after work, too. All meals end with something sweet. All meals. Always. It's a habit that's hard to break once you spend a lot of time eating with French people.

Everything in France is eaten with a fork. Nachos, pizza, burgers, fork, fork, fork. I ignore it and appear rude, oh well. I'm just not eating nachos with a fork. Sorry. Salad is not stabbed, it is folded into a bite-sized piece with your knife and fork before being eaten.

There's a lot of food shaming with French people. I remember being at a party with a table full of *hors d'oeuvres*. (Literally means "outside of the work.) I took a plate and piled on a few of each item, some cheeses, a pâte, some nuts, crackers. Everyone stared at me. Later a friend pulled me aside and said that what I did was *shocking*. I was told that *nobody ever* puts more than 1 or 2 items on a plate at a time in this situation. It wasn't even just odd to her – she called it SHOCKING.

Wait, a sec, I have to make a random comment here. In mentioning the translation of *hors d'oeuvres*, I thought of other words that surprised me. When learning French what struck me as interesting was that *filet mignon* meant cute steak, (*mignon* means cute). And *bonbon*, or good good, meant *candy*.

The word tape in French is *scotch*. *Derrière* means behind. (In the USA it literally means behind, or butt, or backside, which *is* behind you, right?) In French you might use it as... the house is *derrière* the park. (The house is *behind* the park.) A *cul-de-sac* is the neck of a closed bag. A *douche* is a shower. *Souvenir* just means you remember something. Such as – "I remember your crazy aunt." You can see how it took on its meaning in English for items bought to "remember" a trip. And *parfait* means perfect in French. And what could be more perfect than eating an ice cream parfait. That's part of what makes learning languages fun. Lots of discoveries along the journey. The French say goodbye as adieu, in Spanish they'll say adios. To them it simply means goodbye. But I immediately saw it was *A Dieu* and *A Dios*. Both meaning "To God." They are sending you off to go "with God" on your journey.

I digressed again, sorry. I was saying food shaming... Frenchies will always comment about your food... "Oh, you can eat all that?" Or... "Oh that's too much for me." Or..."Oh, I can't eat, I'm still full from lunch." Food shaming. It's a sport in France if you eat differently than they do.

Fizzy beverages are usually not ordered with food. Drinking a Coke or Sprite is a no-no with meals. You can have it before or after, but during a meal -- it's a real eyebrow raiser in France (Doesn't take much!)

Ice is not in big demand in France. Drinking water or soda with no ice is the norm. And they cannot believe we'd drink from 44-ounce cups here. Now that's SHOCKING to them. 44-ounces and lots of ice would kill them. They're happy with 6-ounce drinks at room temperature. Oh, and speaking of drinks... no such thing as a refill in France, each 'refill' is a new separate drink order, a new bill. And where you sit can also cost extra in France. Sitting inside, or outside at the café, will cost more than sitting or standing at the bar.

Last thing, restaurants are not hip with food modifications. All French chefs think their food is perfect. Start asking for no salt, dressing on the side, and extra marinara sauce and you'll probably get Visine added to your food.

If I were in Paris café right now, I could order a *croque Monsieur* (a grilled ham and cheese sandwich) and a *panaché* (half beer, half 7-up) just to have something very French. I'd tip 5%. Tips are not mandatory in France. 5% is the normal tip, unless it's fabulous, *or terrible* service.

Commonly used, proverbs and expressions:

Expression/Proverb	Translation	Meaning
Il me court sur le haricot	He's running on my bean	He's getting on my nerves
Avoir le cafard (J'ai le cafard)	Have the cockroach	Feeling down
En faire tout un fromage	To make cheese out of it	Up the creek without a paddle
Mêle-toi de tes oignons	Mind your onions	Mind your own business
Avaler des couleuvres	Swallow snakes	Someone is lying
Les doigts dans le nez	Fingers in the nose	A piece of cake
Poser un lapin	Put a rabbit	Be stood up
Qui vivra verra	Who lives shall see	Whatever happens, happens
Chacun voit midi à sa porte	One sees noon at his door	It's useless to argue

How to say hello.

We did the whole *bonjour* thing as a must-do greeting, but what about meeting a friend on the street? You might say: *Tiens*! Or *salut*! Which are like hi. Sometimes you'll hear *coucou*, meaning the same, hi, hey, hello there. When answering the phone, or video calls, Zoom, Skype, the French will say *ALLÔ*.

Hit me up.

Here's the famous *COUP*! *Un Coup* means a hit, a blow, a stroke, a punch. Yet you will hear *coup* used all the time, paired up with other words to form commonly used expressions. Pronounced COU without the P of course. It seems odd, but we use it occasionally, consider, "Let me have a hit of your cigarette, a hit of your weed, a hit of acid. (Very '60s here!)

Which coup	When used
Un coup de main	You need a hand, you need help
Jeter un coup d'œil	You need a few seconds, a bit of time
Un coup de fil	Need to make a phone call (Can also say un coup de téléphone)
Boire un coup	Grab a drink, go out for a drink
Tenter le coup	Try to do something even if it's difficult
Un coup de barre	To be fatigued, very tired
Un coup de soleil	When you have a sunburn
En coup de vent	When you're in a hurry
D'un seul coup	At one time

Using the word *coup*, reminds me of *l'air*. These are two little bling words. We reviewed *l'air* about 50 pages ago. It's used, as is the verb *sembler*, to show how something *seems*, or *looks*. You look exotic. *Tu as l'air exotique.* Or he seems nice. *Il a l'air sympa.* Both *l'air* and *un coup* will be used constantly and you should listen for them in fast spoken French.

Word Safari

This is a game that I invented. At least, I don't know anyone else who does this though there could be millions. Ha, ha. I never called it WORD SAFARI till this book, as I wanted a phrase to easily to describe it to you.

I'm always buying foreign language books and picking up foreign magazines to hunt for words in. You can find French books at library book sales, thrifts stores, online sellers. I've got a shelf full of French books I'll never read.

Instead, if I have time, or I'm stuck in an airport, or Dr's waiting room, I'll go on the hunt. Word Safari. All you need is a book, article or magazine, and a few highlighters, pens, or markers. (E-books are great as you can highlight in them too.)

The game is up to you. You might pick ER verbs and go through highlighting all regular ER present tense verbs in the infinitive. Or all ER verbs in *l'imparfait*. (You know what? I really am a nerd. I think I just realized that.)

Next I might take the blue highlighter and stalk out all the times I see *Être with any of her 17* roommates. Or every time I see a liaison. Or the use of future tense. Or every word denoting a color, or size, or number. (*Un* and *une* count here as a number). I know, this is even more cornball than me crying over Julio's music in that Ecuadorian bar, but it's a fun technique to study grammar. It's way more engaging than memorizing verb charts.

As you move along, your page or chapter gets more and more colorful. With a pen you can circle, underline or cross out your various word victims to differentiate them into groups. It's a great way to play with words yet study. Look up anything you don't know. Write it in the notebook, *que tu aimes*. The point is to get more and more familiar with French till your mind sees it as normal, friendly.

Looking at a document in a foreign language is daunting. Lots of strange words, symbols, and accent marks you don't know. The language seems unapproachable. You're an outsider. But once you break it down, you'll see how easy and approachable it is. Getting comfortable with the words, accent marks, apostrophes, liaisons, pronouns and verbs will remove any fear about learning French. You'll be an insider.

Below is a list of ideas to look for when playing WORD SAFARI. Going on these hunts is really important as it'll *actively focus* you on a single aspect of the language. Concept by concept, French will become very familiar and no longer "foreign" to you.

Word Safari ideas:

1. Pick out words that you recognize right away because they're just like English. (30% of English words are said to originate from Latin, as was French).
2. Find words that end in X. Do they represent plural words or not?
3. All future conjugations, used with any personal pronouns.
4. Any place *aller*'s superpower is used as the future, like, *je vais, tu vas,* etc.
5. Find all words that start with a W. That's a trick question. There are none. Weekend and western are used in French but they're borrowed from English. Crazy no? There are no natural French words with a W used anywhere in them.
6. Find words starting with an H. What do they mean?
7. Pick out all reflexive sentences.
8. Find all *cédille* accents. What about the rarer *trëma* accent? Can you find any?
9. Can you see *être* hiding in plain sight anywhere?
10. Find any of the 17 verbs from the House of Être?
11. What about her superpower, *en train de*? Find any?
12. Does anyone *partir* or *sortir* in the document? (Which one means out?)
13. Do you see either of the two know-it-alls in the text?
14. See any reference to sizes? Big, little, long, tall, short, etc. How about colors? Days of the week? Animals? Furniture? Look for items like these to help increase your general vocabulary.
15. Find apostrophes. What letter was removed? Why?
16. Find all *imparfaits.*
17. Highlight verbs with IR endings. RE endings.
18. Can you find any French expressions being used, like *la vache?*

These were a few ideas, but anything you need help with, focus on it and find it in your book, text, or document. When you spend time actively zoomed in, you'll learn quickly. And it'll be way more fun than trying to memorize things by repeating them over and over.

Added bonus, once you get really familiar with all these words by doing word safari, you'll start to see and hear them in movies. I have my TV on just heard someone say "*l'air* "to Kevin Hart. He said, "*Tu as l'air d'un roi.*" (You seem like a king.) These expressions will be so familiar that you'll notice them everywhere. That's the first step, becoming friends with the language. You'll learn the words, hear them spoken, recognize them, and eventually use them. It's a process. Start by just recognizing them. Play Word Safari while you watch movies or TV series with French on. Go thru and watch for bling words, suffixes, future conjugations, *plus* and *mois* being used.etc. You'll be hearing it all!

More "hip, cool, slangy" French words for daily use.

You already know three of the hippest words that you can sprinkle around in your French. The words are ENGLISH. Yes. COOL. SUPER. TOP. They all mean exactly what they say. See or hear something you like, throw out a cool, or super. Top is like the best of something, the top of the line. Just add c'est (it is) to really sound French. *C'est cool. C'est super. C'est top.*

Bordel
Bordel means brothel. Yet for years *bordel* is commonly used to describe a large mess. An example would be: *Range ta chambre. C'est le bordel.* Clean your room. It's a mess.

Baraque
Baraque means shanty, or small house made of planks. Recently the term has been adapted to refer to a house, a *maison* or, as an adjective, it's someone muscular. *On habite dans une grosse baraque avec 10 colocs.* We live in a large house with 10 other people. (Roommates)

BG
These days *BG* is a popular acronym. It stands for *beau gosse,* which means hot guy.

146

BCBG

Another popular acronym, which is the French slang for preppy, is *BCBG Good style, good class. (Bon chic, bon genre).*

Blé, fric, pognon, pèze, balle = **money**

Blé translates as wheat in English. However, figuratively it has become a popular way of referring to money. *Il gagne beaucoup de blé.* He earns a lot of money.

Balle means bullet. Back in the day, *balles* was slang for *francs*, the French currency pre-2002. And when France moved on to the *euro, balles* moved with it and it is still used for money. *J'ai le en acheté au marché pour dix balles.* I bought them at the market for 10 euros.

Bouffer = **food**

To *bouffer* means to balloon-up in size. It's now the go-to-word to re-place manger (to eat) in everyday speech. *La bouffe* is food. *Je suis allé acheter de la bouffe.* I went to buy some food.

Metro – boulot – dodo = **metro, work, sleep.**

You'll hear this 3 word expression a lot from Parisians describing their typi-cal daily work grind: *Metro,* (to get to work) *boulot,* (at work) *dodo,* (baby talk for sleeping.)

Vachement and *tellement*.

You can use these two words everywhere for emphasis. Basically, they mean *very* or sooooo. *C'est vachement cool.* That is soooo cool. *C'est tellement super.* That is soooo super. This wine is soooo good. That photo is soooo interesting. (If you noticed that *vachement* has the word cow, or *vache* in it, you're right. It means cowly. It is cowly cool! You might remember the ex-pression we looked at earlier: *Oh, la vache.* The French might have a thing for cows.

Un mec, un type	a guy
Une nana, une meuf	a girl
Un flic, keuf, poulet	a cop
Taffe, bosse, boulot	to work, a job
Reuch, douloureuse	Expensive
Radin	Cheap
Putain!	F%#k! (orig. from whore, today's *favorite* French swear word!)
Ah merde	oh shit!
Une salop	a louse, a worthless person, creep… bitch

Shhh… quiet please.

Don't speak too loudly. It's very American (I can say that, I'm American) and to the French it's very *gauche*. The French are more discreet. They do not want to overhear your phone conversation, and you won't be overhearing theirs.

Speaking of speaking.

There is an unspoken rule, well, actually, it's a spoken rule: you do not use the informal *TU* in formal *VOUS* settings. It's considered to be rude and shows disrespect. *Tu* and *vous* both mean YOU but are from two different classes. *Tu* belongs to the familiar, it's for your buddies, addressing friends, pets, family, peers, children. *Vous* is reserved for the more reserved… grand-parents, business associates, strangers you stop on the street to ask directions, store employees, teachers, your doctor, President Macron, the Pope, etc. If you're not sure if it's *vous* or *tu*, default to *vous* to be safe.

How do you break out from speaking in the formal *vous* form into the friend-ly *tu* form? You can simply ask. *Est-ce que on peut se **tutoyer**?* Or shorter, *on peut se **tutoyer**?* (Yes, there's a word for it.) ***Tutoyer** is* used to switch from

148

the formal to the familiar. I've never had anyone say no. For me, and for many others who've learned languages on the streets, using the formal *vous*

is very difficult. Most of us have learned to speak listening to friends and peers, who always use the *tu* form when speaking to us. *Tu* becomes ingrained in our brains. We have to stay really alert to speak in the *vous* form. (It's my number one problem in speaking all romance languages.)

Paris is not France.

Never ask someone in Paris what part of Paris they're from. It's usually an insult as the person might be from Nice, Normandy, or Nemours. Paris is not France. There is a small snobbery that goes on between Paris towards other provinces, and *vise versa*. The total area of France is 211,209 square miles, making France slightly smaller than two Colorados put together. It's smaller than the state of Texas at 268,820 square miles of area. French nationals feel that every region in France is to be admired, none to be ignored because of the big *cité,* Paris.

In NYC we have the term 'bridge and tunnel people.' These are the people who live outside of the borough of Manhattan and have to get to the city by bridges or tunnels. There's a snobbery, a feeling of superiority from many Manhattanites towards the bridge and tunnel people. Same deal in Paris with out-of-towners.

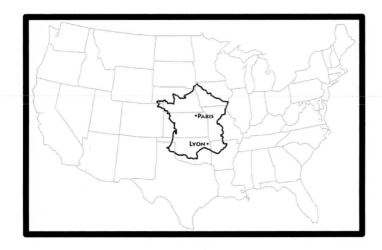

All aboard. Time to get back on the train.

Ahh, welcome back to familiar territory. Here's some *déjà vu* words we've already studied. Familiar turf. Let's see if you remember this. (Funny, we use *déjà vu* in English to describe some mystic, psychic experience, a strange feeling of having been somewhere before. In French it's used daily, its real meaning is a very non cryptic, simple: I *saw it*.)

Back to familiar territory. Here are some big, useful takeaways from our past studies here in the pages together.

AVOIR BESOIN DE

We didn't look at the marriage of BESOIN and DE yet.. Don't mean to spring yet another new thing on you but AVOIR BESOIN DE is something you'll NEED TO know. And it means – need to. And the two words go together. I *have besoin de* explain this. Notice how we say *need to:* I need to eat. They need to move. We need to find the car. Saying I need eat, they need move, or, we need find the car isn't cool. Same with *besoin de* – the two words go together. Watch for that, you'll see them paired up all the time. So you *need to* remember that *besoin de* is also a team.

Hold on a sec, I know I sprung yet *more* info on you there. You might be thinking – when does it end? Does it end? Can I deal with the nonstop input?

Maybe you're thinking *Stop already -- I cannot do this anymore*! But wait -- here's the good news… in this little book, you've got everything you need to speak French. To communicate fully in a new language. And it's really not that much! It's work, sure, but you didn't have to take years of college, move to France for a year, hire private tutors. Even learning half of this info will get you out and about spewing French whenever you need to, or want to (There's our *"need to."*)

Point is – yes, there was a ton of new stuff on every page, but that's all you need to speak pretty good French. (There's our *pretty*.)

Looking at the big picture – it's really not that much when the outcome is that *you speak a new language*. That's incredible. French! Boom! That might be life changing for you.

So don't give up. Go through your notebook, review your writings, flip through this book, play Word Safari, learn vocabulary – and you'll get super familiar with the language. Watch Netflix, listen well, you'll hear all the words you know, like, *l'air, besoin de, il faut, je suis, il y a*, etc. You'll be surprised how much you've picked up. Use your remote control, pause the TV over and over as you watch. Use subtitles. And BOOM! You'll hear and see words you know, you'll understand more and more. It's really not that much. Of course you can continue studying till you can write French novels, if you want, but this is really all you need to communicate well in French – anywhere! Any time. Congrats! Rant over.

Where were we? Oh, yes, more info…

EN TRAIN DE
Ahh, the fabulous train, rating in at half a verb tense. This is the ING work-horse of the French world. What do trains do? The train is GOING. The train is LEAVING. The train is MOVING. ING. ING. ING. I am eating. We are leaving. You are deciding. He is giving. They are winning. ING. ING. ING. If you're doing something you're on the famous train. *Je suis en train de manger. On est en train de partir. Vous êtes en train de décider. Il est en train de donner. Il est en train de gagner.*

JE VIENS DE
Literally it means "I came from." But it's used as our "just." I *just* finished eating. He *just* found his book. She *just* left the house. They *just* called look-ing for you. I *just* added up the price. Anywhere we use "just" in English,

which is all day, every day, you will use *venir de. Je viens de manger. Tu viens de parler. Paul vient de décider.*

IL Y A

Here's the 3 little bling words that add up to mean *there is* or *there are. Il y a 3 chiens. Il y a un gummy bear sur la table. Il y a du temps pour décider.*

EST-CE QUE

Add this before anything in French and it's suddenly becomes a question. There is a doctor there, (*Il y a un médecin là*) becomes *is there a doctor there?* If you add *est-ce que* first. **Est-ce qu' il y a un médecin là?** Remember this as just one oddly spelled word, not 3 tiny groups of mostly vowels. EST-CE QUE (Pronounced S-qu). *Un médecin* or *un docteur* can be used above.

STU

This is our lovely little guy *TU*. He's always carting around an S so we've renamed him Stu just to remember the S when spelling *TU* in conjugations.

JE VAIS

If you can't remember how to say something in the future tense, *aller* is always there to help you out. *Je vais* is -- I'm going to. I'm going to take the test. *Je vais faire le test.* He's going to find it. *Il va le trouver.* She's gonna look silly. *Elle va avoir l'air ridicule.* (See *l'air*, next)

L'AIR

This is the vivid way the French say " it looks like", or " it seems". She looks silly. He seems smart. The cake looks stale. The water seems dirty. This is *l'air* at work. *Elle a l'air ridicule. Il a l'air intelligent. Le gateau a l'air rassis. L'eau a l'air sale.* You will hear and use this expression all day once you get used to it.

TRUC

This is a must-have word. It's used to mean *thing, thing-a-majig, whatcha-ma-call-it.* It's great when you don't know a word, stick in *truc*. Like, what is this thing? Do you have any more of this thing? How much is this thing? I like that thing. Endless uses. When you don't know a word, throw in *truc* to replace the missing "thing". And of course, people will usually mention the word you need when replying. (*Truc* literally means trick, so you are saying for example, "How much is this trick?" But it's used non-stop to mean *thing*.) The word *machin* can also be used, just like truc, to replace *thing*.

Another spell coming on...

And – just to remind you – we learned how to spell the word *FUTUR* wrong. *Futor*. Remember? The 0, the ONT, used for the *ILS* and *ELLES* in the future tense.

CA-CHING!

Here are some money saving tips for you. First, you CAN drink the water in Paris. While many restaurants want you to buy a bottle of expensive bottled water (often the price of this book – in paperback) you can order a FREE carafe of water. Fresh, great Paris water, one of the top- rated tap waters in the world. You'll save a fortune. (Most Americans know this, but the French flip when I tell them that EVIAN is NAÏVE spelled backwards.)

And back to tipping in France. I shoulda mentioned that French waiters don't rely on tips. Unlike American waiters, French wait staff get regular salaries and benefits. So you don't have to feel guilty about not tipping, or not tipping much. I was in the famous Deux Maggots café with a Parisian friend and the total bill was 58 euros. ($63.00 USD). I paid the bill and my friend insisted on paying the tip. She put down ONE EURO. ONE? WHAT? And it was well received. No dirty looks from the waiter, no odd looks from fellow diners… nothing. It was a good example of the norm for tipping in France. Ca-ching!

Movies, TV, and Word Safari.

Not much of a reader? Don't have many books written in French? Movies with subtitles are just as good. Grab the remote and get ready to hit PAUSE. Watch for words you know as they go by. Pause on sentences. Take a good look. See any familiar faces? *L'air* may show up five times. *Il y a* again and again. *En train de?* Yep, a lot. You'll start to see them and recognize them.

This is FRENCH becoming friendly. This is French working for YOU! Languages can be great fun. Go on the hunt with Word Safari. It's always great when you spot a familiar face in the crowd.

English has a very famous ER ending, too.

While the French have 1000's of ER verb endings, in English there's a superstar ER ending, too -- an all important ending that the French don't have. It's the ER of *"comparative adjectives."* These are the ER endings that compare things: Faster, sweeter, nearer, taller, harder, longer, pinker, smarter, etc. Without our ER endings, the French have to go another route.

In French to compare, first you have to add MORE (***PLUS***), or LESS (***MOIN***). Things are more big, more smart, more tall. Or they may be less big, less smart, less tall. ***Plus*** or ***moin.*** If it's more, first you add *PLUS.* (pronounced plu). *PLUS* fast, (*plus rapide*), *PLUS* sweet, (*plus doux*), PLUS big, (*plus grand*).

If you want it to be less, add *MOIN* first. (pronounced mua). *MOIN* fast, (*moin rapide*), *MOIN* sweet, (*moin doux*), *MOIN* big, (*moin grand*).

English uses this technique too, like the word *expensive*. There's no "expensiver." We say it's *more expensive*, or *less expensive*. Also things can be a lot *more fun* or a lot *less fun,* but they're not described as funner.
These two simple words *plus* and *moin* are great additions to your notebook, *que tu aimes. (*I hope you do *aimes* your notebook.)

The Pareto Principle

This is the famous 80/20 rule. In 1906 an Italian economist, Vilfredo Pareto had an observation. He realized that 20% of the population in Italy owned 80% of the land. As he researched further, he discovered many other 80/20 principles all around him. Basically 80% of the output is created by 20% of input. Today it can be said that 80% of the crimes were being committed by 20% of the criminals. 80% of the world's pollution originates from 20% of the industries. 80% of workplace results are achieved by 20% of the employees. 80% of a company's revenue comes from just 20% of its customers. The 80/20 principle is used in everything, from interior design… to social media, it's EVERYWHERE. (In design, if you decorate 80% of a room in neutral colors, you're smart to use bright colors for 20%. In social media, 80% of the traffic is generated by 20% of the posts.)

Let's look at the Pareto principle and languages. Basically 80% of what you'll use and need to speak well, is acquired by 20% of your studies. 80% of your improvement is reached through 20% of what you learned.

So watch what you learn. Make that 20% you're learning super valuable. Don't spend 80% of your time wasted on things you need 20% of the time. Spend your time learning what you really need. Learn the top 100 or 500 words used in your target languages. Learn the top verbs. The most used expressions. The most valued bling words. Make your learning count. If you're not doing horoscopes don't waste your time learning the words retrograde, Quincunx Opposition or Sextile Trine. Focus on what you need. In this book, I've tried to include only the bling, suffixes, verbs and vocabulary most needed, most heard, and most used. If you were to learn everything in this book, you'd be speaking really great French. It's maybe 20%, or less, of what you can learn to speak good French, but over 80% of the time, I think it's all you'll need to converse very well.

One more trip to Frenchville.

Frenchville can be hard to reach; a.distant place off the beaten path. When walking down the street, you can easily be daydreaming instead. Or listening to music… or talking on the phone. To arrive in Frenchville you must decide to talk to yourself about your surroundings in French: describe the tall green tree, the big white house, the thin lady in the red dress at Starbucks. Unless it's fun, it can be hard to arrive at that special land called Frenchville.

So how do you make it more fun or more important than listening to your favorite music in your earbuds as you go? First, you have to remember WHY you're learning French. You have to be motivated. Can you picture the end result? Are you in St Barts ordering a *mojito* in French? Are you shocking your new in-laws by speaking to them in their native French language. Are you excelling in your French class and your teacher is kinda stunned? Can you see yourself in a Paris bake shop eating a croissant during your long awaited trip to France? Always remember – you are the boss here, it is all about YOU. No language is the boss. You decide what you need to learn… as you need to learn it… at YOUR pace.

Keep it fun. Set goals. Use lots of bling words this week and new words the next. (*De temps en temps* the big green tree is growing. It's *plus grand*). Then check them off in this book, or your notebook. Use tons of suffixes one week. The big white house is *magnifique*. Introduce some of the 17 guests from the House of Être. I *arrivé* at the end of the street. (Try to say these whole sentences in French, of course). And don't forget to add sounds, smells. Do you hear a bird chirping? Smell a bar-b-que grilling? It's all more color for your world.

Make it all a quiz, a game. Go through your list of suffixes, for example, and check off the ones you've used. Check off the residents of the House of *Être* as you get more acquainted with them. Pick out new verb roots you haven't used and add them to your Frenchville sentences. I would like to *manger* that bird (No, not that.) Try out future tenses. I will *parlerai* with that woman tomorrow. (As soon as you see that **R** in the verb, and the whole root is there, like in *parlerai*, can figure out right away it's talking about the future.)

Think of your notebook, *que tu aimes*, as your best friend. It's the two of you. A great team. Let him (or her) help you. Rely on him/her to be there to assist you. Write down thoughts, tricks you've discovered to help you remember words, new vocabulary. Don't leave home without him/her. This is your best friend for learning French.

As you go, start adding things you will hear and use ALL DAY in French. *En train de, l'air, je vien de, il faut.* You will hear these words 100 times a day by French speakers, or on your French Netflix shows. That coffee has *l'air* of being weak. (seems) I *vien de* eat at my friend's house. (Just, or came from) *Il faut* que you tell me the truth. (You must, or you should) I am *en train de* visit Frenchville. (visiting). Use these words over and over, apply them to everything and anything you can. (Don't forget *il y a* and *est-ce que*, think of them as just funny spelled words meaning one thing each.) Include all the new words and expressions, piece by piece,

Check all your newly learned items them off in this book, or in your note-book. Have a friend quiz you on them. They can go through the lists and ask you what these words mean. (Bet them! "I'll buy you a Frappucino if I can't get 30 correct!")

Go to Frenchville. Visit as often as possible. Have a foreign Preply.com study buddy you can talk to later about your trip into Frenchville, repeat the words you used. This is how you will adjust to the common words used in French all day. This will all help you learn to speak French, if you are not already living in a French speaking world.

Just who is Ann Landers?

Some of you may remember a syndicated columnist named Ann Landers. (Did you know her sister was Dear Abby?) It was back when the bulging Sunday newspaper weighed three pounds and everyone read 'the paper' to find out what was going on in the world.

Ann answered questions from readers about how to handle their own life sit-uations. What to do with a cheating spouse? A runaway kid? A spying neighbor? From your barking pet, to your bright pink corvette, Ann had an opinion about it.

But she said something I always remembered. A female wrote her asking if she should go to college to become a lawyer. The woman was older and said she wouldn't graduate till she was 71. Should she bother? I still remember Ann's response. She said "Of course! You're gonna be 71 *anyway*, you might as well be a lawyer then, too. You'll be a lot happier, prouder, and it's all around better for you."

Do you get the connection with French, or anything you want to achieve? This year is gonna go by anyway – at the end of it -- you might as well speak French. You can easily achieve that. You might as well, right? Put the time in. It's not always easy. It's work, yes. But it can be fun, too. Keep it fun.

Don't stress. DON'T STRESS. You can do it. And by the end of a year, you could have the whole new world of French wide open for you.

Or not.

It's up to you. I say – go for it! The YOU 12 months from now will really love yourself for it!

Champagne time...

That's it. That's all I can think of to share with you to get you up and running in spoken French. I'm 100% positive that I'll think of 1,000 other things as soon as I put this book up on Amazon, but such is life. *C'est la vie.*

Now, if you're confused in areas, and not sure you're getting it – that's the way learning languages is. Don't fret. Remember, this is a foreign language, so it's *foreign* to everything you've learned about your own language. It does take time. Stay with it. And remember, while you're studying, you're not alone; there are millions of people all over the world, at the same time, also learning a new language. You're in lots of great company. Stay with us. And never forget – you're in charge. Language was made for YOU to communicate. It works for YOU. Without YOU it doesn't even exist! So carry on at YOUR pace. We're all glad to know you're here!

Now, the toast... when you take the metal wire cage, *le muselet*, off the top of the champagne bottle, (always 6 turns), be very careful not to let the cork escape. Unless you're celebrating a win at the Gran Prix by splashing bubbly at the crowd, you don't want a drop of champagne spilling from the bottle. *Ce n'est pas cool.*

Place your palm over the cork to prevent it from flying out and turn the bottle, yes, *turn the bottle, not the cork.* Keep your palm pressed against the cork and turn the bottle as you wind the cork out.

Now, tilt the glass towards the bottle and pour just one inch. Let the sparkling suds calm down, then add more. You don't want a glass full of foam, pour slowly.

Okay, now we both have a glass of bubbly. Let's toast to you, to thank you for reading this book, a labor of love (and hate.) Wishing you a lifetime full of success at learning and speaking French.

And I'm raising a toast to me, for taking on grammar, my most hated subject on earth, to try to share my little cheats.

I hope you've been helped by my efforts. I've tried my best to relay my tips, tricks, secrets and hacks, and tried to make French a more friendly language.

Here's to you, and to the Kumbaya Clan, the French Academy, and to all the diamond thieves of the world... *À votre santé*. Bottoms up! MERCI!

P.S. If you've reached here – you're a champ. If my little guide has helped you -- and I soooo (*vachement, tellement*) hope it did -- please write a review. I'd so appreciate it, they're really important, especially for small independent publishers like me. ☺

If you have any questions, if there's anything not clear, or you have any comments about the book, or even find a typo that bothers you -- here's my vintage addy: Cougy@aol.com. I do still get mail there, and I will respond.

Again, thank you for taking the time to read this book. I'm honored.

ONE YEAR LATER...

Hello again,

Yes -- I thought I was done too.

It's about a year after I last revised this book *un peu* and we toasted with champagne. But I'm always playing with the concept, trying to improve it. I thought these following puzzles and questions might be a fun way to learn some new words.

Also, add the correct accents and meanings to the upcoming word lists to help you remember them.

Remy

1.

FIND: **MEANING:**

AGACER

AMER

APPORT

CARRE

CRUELLE

EMINCEE

IDOLE

INFLUX

JINGLE

NIVEAU

PLONGER

REVOIR

TRUQUE

1.

F	I	J	T	O	F	H	D	Y	A	J	U	G	A
Y	D	U	Q	E	S	A	H	E	E	I	J	V	M
P	O	R	F	R	L	E	G	A	G	N	K	B	E
E	L	A	P	P	O	R	T	A	U	G	H	S	R
F	E	V	M	R	R	X	S	H	C	L	D	W	Z
B	P	V	A	P	N	W	A	L	N	E	L	I	N
R	I	C	C	R	U	E	L	L	E	T	R	P	F
M	N	A	S	Y	Z	G	U	V	W	R	R	L	L
W	F	X	K	R	Q	A	S	X	D	U	I	O	A
M	L	W	E	E	P	H	E	E	Q	C	N	E
S	U	L	A	V	R	U	K	H	G	U	F	G	S
X	X	E	I	O	S	R	E	L	G	E	V	E	S
Q	P	N	X	I	G	Q	E	D	P	F	Y	R	V
P	I	Y	E	R	A	E	M	I	N	C	E	E	A

Remember H is not pronounced. Lots of words resembling English, but just the endings, suffixes are changed. ALLER'S gang is here, with some from his ER verb group, too.

2.

FIND:	**MEANING:**
ADOREE	
ARRIVER	
CAPRE	
CONFITE	
CONNECTER	
COUPLE	
DEFRISER	
DESIRABLE	
EMBRASER	
ESKIMO	
HOTELIERE	
HUIT	
IMPULSIF	
MAGNIFIQUE	

2.

```
M  I  J  C  O  N  N  E  C  T  E  R  G  P
Y  D  U  E  L  L  E  T  R  P  F  J  V  M
T  W  Z  G  U  V  W  R  R  L  L  K  B  E
E  I  Q  A  S  X  D  U  I  E  A  H  S  O
M  E  U  P  H  E  C  Q  C  L  E  D  M  M
B  P  R  H  K  O  G  U  E  P  S  A  I  I
R  I  S  R  N  L  G  E  V  U  S  R  G  K
M  N  G  F  E  D  R  F  Y  O  V  R  P  S
W  F  I  E  M  O  N  C  E  C  A  I  N  E
M  T  W  E  D  M  L  R  E  E  P  V  Y  E
E  U  L  A  V  D  E  I  O  J  L  E  S  M
X  X  E  I  O  R  Q  C  N  O  A  R  V  A
Q  P  N  C  I  P  R  E  G  K  E  J  I  G
R  B  P  S  U  K  O  G  U  E  P  S  A  N
W  R  E  H  O  T  E  L  I  E  R  E  R  I
N  D  N  G  F  E  M  B  R  A  S  E  R  F
O  D  V  P  R  X  M  S  S  Y  T  H  W  I
U  B  E  F  I  S  L  U  P  M  I  U  U  Q
B  X  X  E  I  O  R  Q  C  N  O  A  R  U
T  B  X  A  V  L  G  H  F  G  D  O  U  E
```

Had to throw some superheroes and bad boys in, I kinda missed them. Don't forget to add the accent marks – you know ETRE hates losing her crown. And... there's a slang word, can you spot it?

3.

FIND: **MEANING:**

ALLER

AVOIR

BIEN

BOUFFER

ETRE

CONNAITRE

SAVOIR

SKIER

PARLER

VENDRE.

3.

```
E  P  M  I  U  U  Q  L  L  R  E  I  K  S
Q  C  N  O  A  R  U  E  A  H  S  O  G  P
H  O  G  D  O  U  E  L  E  D  W  M  V  M
P  N  Z  G  G  U  E  P  B  I  E  N  E  Y
A  N  Q  A  S  X  M  N  G  F  E  D  R  F
R  A  U  P  H  A  W  F  I  E  M  O  N  C
L  I  R  H  K  O  V  T  E  L  I  E  R  E
E  T  S  R  N  L  V  O  U  S  R  G  E  E
R  R  G  F  E  E  R  F  I  O  V  R  P  R
W  E  I  E  N  O  N  C  E  R  A  I  N  T
M  T  E  D  I  E  R  R  I  P  V  Y  E
E  U  R  B  R  A  B  I  R  F  L  E  S  M
X  E  M  S  S  Y  T  O  W  I  A  R  V  A
A  P  L  U  P  M  I  V  U  Q  E  J  I  G
R  L  R  Q  C  N  O  A  R  F  P  S  A  N
W  R  L  H  F  G  D  O  U  E  F  E  R  I
G  D  N  E  F  E  M  B  R  A  S  E  R  F
O  D  V  P  R  X  M  S  S  Y  T  H  Q  P
```

Food for thought. Hopefully you don't eat lapin, and we know Macaron was not the president of France. :) BTW, lapin is never mentioned, eaten, or brought aboard any French ships. It's bad luck. (One word here isn't food. See it?)

4.

FIND:	MEANING:

AIL

BAGUETTE

CAROTTE

CASSOULET

CREPES

DOMMAGE

FROMAGE

HARICOT

LAPIN

MACARON

POIRE

4.

```
B  P  M  I  U  U  Q  L  L  R  E  I  K  S
Q  A  O  O  A  R  U  E  A  H  S  O  G  E
H  O  G  I  O  U  E  L  E  D  W  M  V  P
P  N  Z  U  R  U  E  P  B  I  E  N  A  E
A  N  Q  A  E  E  M  N  G  F  E  S  R  R
R  A  U  P  H  T  W  F  I  E  S  O  N  C
L  I  R  C  K  O  T  T  E  L  I  E  R  E
E  L  S  C  A  L  V  E  V  U  S  R  G  E
R  R  G  F  A  S  S  T  O  C  I  R  A  H
W  E  I  E  N  U  S  T  E  R  A  I  N  T
L  T  E  D  I  E  S  O  R  I  P  V  Y  E
A  U  R  B  R  A  B  R  U  F  L  E  S  M
P  E  M  S  S  Y  T  A  W  L  A  R  V  A
I  P  L  U  P  M  I  C  U  Q  E  J  I  G
N  L  R  E  G  A  M  O  R  F  P  T  A  N
W  R  L  H  F  G  D  O  U  E  F  E  R  I
P  O  R  A  C  A  M  B  R  A  S  E  Y  F
O  D  V  P  R  X  M  S  S  Y  T  H  R  P
```

Grammar's back. Can you tell by the endings what tenses these verbs are referring to? Verb endings do the heavy lifting. They're there to tell you the who, what, and where about their verbs. (If you can't figure it out, don't worry. It's a process, slowly but surely.) Hey – our buddy STU's here.

You can see just by the endings that a few words are not conjugations.

5.

FIND:	**MEANING:**
AURAS	
AVEC	
DONC	
FERMER	
MANGERAI	
MANGER	
PARLAIS	
PARLES	
PUNITIF	
QUAND	
TROUVERONT	

5.

I	P	Y	L	V	Q	V	B	S	R	E	I	K	S
W	A	A	S	S	U	O	C	I	R	S	O	G	E
H	R	N	U	S	A	E	Z	A	I	W	D	V	P
P	L	I	E	S	N	R	I	V	V	O	N	A	E
O	A	D	A	B	D	U	F	E	N	E	S	R	R
R	I	S	Y	T	A	W	L	C	R	S	F	N	C
L	S	P	M	I	C	E	Q	E	J	I	E	R	E
E	L	G	A	M	O	R	F	P	T	S	R	G	E
R	R	G	N	A	U	R	A	S	C	I	M	A	H
M	A	N	G	E	R	S	T	E	L	A	E	N	T
L	T	E	E	E	S	O	R	I	P	R	Y	E
A	U	R	R	R	P	U	N	I	T	I	F	S	M
P	E	N	A	S	Y	T	A	W	L	A	S	V	A
I	A	L	I	P	M	I	C	U	Q	E	E	I	G
M	L	R	E	G	A	M	O	R	F	P	L	A	N
W	R	L	H	F	G	D	O	U	E	F	R	R	I
N	O	R	A	C	A	M	B	R	A	S	A	R	F
T	R	O	U	V	E	R	O	N	T	T	P	R	Q

Important basic words to increase vocabulary. Don't forget about Word Safari. You can easily get inexpensive French books to play with from Ebay, Facebook marketplace, local library sales, etc. (Don't forget to add the accents marks to all these word lists.)

6.

FIND:	**MEANING:**

AUCUN

CELUI

COUTE

DEPUIS

DESOLE

LEUR

PENDANT

QUELLE

RAISON

RIEN

SUITE

6.

```
I S S L V Q V B S R E I K S
W P U S S U O C I R S O G E
H R I U S A E Z E I W D V J
P L T E S N R I V L O N A E
O O E A B D U F E N U S R R
R I S Y T A W L C R S I N C
L S P M I C E Q E J I E R E
E L G A M O N O S I A R P E
R R G U A U U A S C I M E H
M A S C O U T E E L A E N T
L E E U E E S O R I P R D E
A U L N R N U N I T I F A M
P E N O S Y E A W L A S N L
I A L I S M I I U Q E I T G
M L R R G E M O R F P U A N
W R U H F G D O U E F P R A
N E R A C A M B R A S E Q F
L K Q U E L L E N T T D R O
```

7.

FIND: **MEANING:**

ASSEZ

BANLIEUE

COLLINE

COMPTE

ECRAN

ETAGE

MECHANT

RUELLE

SIECLE

VENTRE

```
M  S  W  L  P  Q  M  B  S  R  E  I  K  S
W  P  U  S  S  E  O  A  I  R  S  O  G  E
R  R  Q  U  C  A  E  N  E  T  A  G  E  J
P  W  T  H  D  N  R  L  V  L  O  N  A  R
O  S  A  A  B  D  U  I  E  N  U  S  R  U
M  N  S  Y  T  A  W  E  C  R  S  I  N  E
T  S  P  M  S  C  E  U  E  J  I  E  R  L
E  L  G  S  M  O  N  E  S  I  A  N  P  L
R  R  E  U  A  U  U  A  S  C  I  I  E  E
M  Z  S  C  O  U  T  E  E  L  A  L  N  T
E  E  E  U  O  E  S  O  R  I  P  L  D  E
R  U  L  N  R  M  U  N  I  T  I  O  A  M
T  E  N  O  S  Y  P  A  W  L  A  C  N  L
N  A  L  I  S  M  I  T  U  Q  E  I  T  G
E  L  E  C  R  A  N  E  E  F  P  U  A  N
V  R  U  H  F  G  S  I  E  C  L  E  R  I
N  E  R  A  C  A  M  B  R  A  S  E  R  F
```

8.

<u>**FIND**</u>:   <u>**MEANING**</u>:

CONSEILLE

COURANT

DETAND

DISPONIBLE

EPUISE

MAUVAISE

PIRE

PROFITEZ

RIGOLES

SINON

TAILLE

8.

```
B  C  W  P  I  R  E  B  S  D  E  E  K  G
D  O  U  S  S  E  O  A  N  R  L  O  G  E
R  N  Q  U  C  A  E  A  E  L  A  G  E  J
P  S  T  H  D  N  T  L  I  L  O  N  A  R
R  E  A  A  B  E  U  A  E  N  U  S  R  U
O  I  S  Y  D  A  T  E  C  R  S  I  N  E
F  L  P  M  S  C  E  C  O  U  R  A  N  T
I  L  G  S  M  O  N  E  S  I  A  N  P  L
T  E  E  U  A  U  P  A  E  C  I  R  E  E
E  Z  S  C  O  U  T  E  L  L  A  I  N  T
Z  E  E  U  I  E  S  E  B  I  P  G  D  E
R  U  L  S  R  M  S  N  I  T  I  O  A  M
T  E  E  O  S  I  P  A  N  L  A  L  N  L
U  A  L  I  A  M  I  T  O  Q  E  E  T  G
Q  L  E  V  K  A  N  E  P  F  P  S  A  N
V  R  U  H  F  G  S  I  S  C  L  E  R  I
N  A  R  A  C  G  M  B  I  A  S  E  R  M
M  R  N  O  N  I  S  E  D  T  X  D  R  Q
```

This next section is a bit more intermediate, but if you feel like it, here are some questions you can answer and fill in the blanks. You'll have to do research to find some of these facts, and to understand any new vocabulary here.

If you're not in the mood to answer here, you can use these questions for Word Safari. Go through and pick out all the plural words. Look at the sentences they're in, you'll see lots in the sentence matches its form both in plural and in gender. (Example, part of question 28 from below: *Quelles* **sont les deux plus** *grosses* planetes... See how everything became plural and feminine to match?)

Playing Word Safari you can try to spot any root verbs, tenses, sticky rice, bad boys, and words with suffixes you recognize. (I.e., you'll see words like quantité = quantity, mouvement = movement, and artistique = artistic, etc.)

Circle apostrophes jumping in to help the weak vowels.

Quel, quels, quelle and *quelles* are repeated everywhere. Plus a few *qui's*. What is being used and why?

There are lots more to discover if you're in the mood. You can figure out many of the questions too without looking them up. Just like learning to speak, you'll recognize a few words and get the gist of what's being said. Slowly you'll pick up more and more words and *voilà* – you're speaking and understanding French. That's how we all learn, piece-by-piece. Remember – word, sentence, paragraph, page. So play around here and locate any words you'll find useful.

If you do respond to the questions, try to reply in French. You'll find all the answers at the end of the book.

1. L'architecte de l'église de la Sagrada Familia, à Barcelone?

2. Cette actrice espagnole a tourné dans plusieurs films de Pedro Almodovar.

3. Sport sur un ring ?

4. Comment écrire 93 ?

5. Un des fondateurs des Rolling Stones ? (Mort en 1969)

6. Un film de Michael Mann, 2004, avec Tom Cruise and Jamie Foxx ?

7. Cet homme de'État Romain conquit la Gaule.

8. Un fleuve des États-Unis passant à New York.

9. Par qui fut popularisé le cacao ?

10. Quel pays s'appelle le pays des lapin ?

11. La piste pour avions ?

12. Le peintre Kandinsky fit partie de ce mouvement artistique du XX siecle ?

13. Combien de pays sont sur la frontière avec la france?

14. Boston est la capitale de cet État de Nouvelle-Angleterre, au nord-est des États-Unis ?

15. Quand les premiers dinosaures seraient-ils apparus sur terre ? 900, 230, ou 600 millions d'annees ?

16. Une rotation de la terre dure environ...24 heures, 4 semaines, ou 365 jours ?

17. Parmi ces villes, laquelle se situe le plus au nord de la France ? (Marseille, Lyon, Bordeaux, Gre-noble ?)

18. Quel est le fleuve le plus long deLa France ? (La Loire, La Seine, Le Rhone, La Moselle ?)

19. Quelle personnalité a été assassinée à New York le 21 février 1965 ?

20. A quelle tribu d'Indiens appartenait Geronimo ?

21. Quel groupe de hard-rock est emmené par *les frères Young ?*

22. Quel group a été créé par Annie Lenox?

23. Qu'est-ce qu'un bichon ?

24. Quel animal était Flipper dan le série télévisée ?

25. Amy Winehouse, dans quelle ville est-elle née ?

26. En quelle année, le Mur de Berlin est-il tombe ?

27. Combien font 999 x 998 ?

28. Quelles sont les deux plus grosses planètes du système solaire ?

29. Quel métal alcalin est symbolisé par la lettre K ?

30. À quel auteur doit-on le roman MOBY DICK ?

31. Quelle est la valeur approximative de Pi(**Π)** ?

32. Qui a réalisé le film HANNIBAL?

33. Qui a écrit la série Twilight?

34. Quelle est la nationalité de Kenzo, fondateur de la marque Kenzo ?

35. En quelle année le droit de vote a-t-il été accordé aux femmes ?

36. Le mot CORAZON en espagnol, que signifie en francais ?

37. Quel acteur célèbre s'est donné la mort en Juillet 2014 ?

38. Dans quel sport s'est illustré Michael Jordan ?

39. A qui doit-on le nom du fruit clémentine ?

40. Quel est le terme francais pour e-mail ?

41. Qui a réalisé le film 4 JUILLET ?

42. Quelle est la capitale du Canada ?

43. Quelle est la capitale de Pérou ?

44. Quel groupe a interprété la chanson Easy On Me ?

ANSWERS :

1 Antoni Gaudi
2 Penélope Cruz
3 La boxe
4 Quatre-vingt-treize
5 Brian Jones
6 Collatéral
7 Jules César
8 L'Hudson
9 Christophe Colomb
10 Espagne
11 La ville de Londres
12 Abstrait
13 8
14 Le Massachusetts
15 230
16 24 heures
17 Lyon
18 La Loire
19 Malcolm X
20 Les Apaches
21 AC/DC
22 Les Eurythmiques
23 Un chien
24 Le dauphin
25 À Londres
26 1989
27 997,002
28 Sont Jupiter et Saturne
29 Le potassium
30 Herman Melville
31 3.14
32 Ridley Scott
33 Stephenie Meyer
34 Japonais
35 1944
36 Le coeur
37 Robin Williams
38 Le basket
39 Le Frère Clément
40 Le courriel
41 Oliver Stone
42 Ottawa
43 Lima
44 Adele

Other books by this author:

Orphans of Katrina: Inside the World's Biggest Animal Rescue (Non-fiction)

The Really Red Rabbit (A picture book)

The Writer and the Quail (A comedy novella. *BTW: This is my favorite book*. A must read.)

Rios Favelas: An Insider Uncovers the Myths, the Music, the Murders (Non-fiction)

Made in United States
North Haven, CT
13 February 2023

32536205R10114